# WHAT ARE THEY SAYING ABOUT LUKE?

# What Are They Saying About Luke?

*Mark Allan Powell*

PAULIST PRESS
*New York/Mahwah*

Powell, Mark Allan, 1953-
    What are they saying about Luke? / by Mark Allan Powell.
        p.   cm.
    Includes bibliographical references
    ISBN 0-8091-3111-0 : $5.95 (est.)
        1. Bible. N.T. Luke—Criticism, interpretation, etc.  2. Bible.
N.T. Luke—Criticism, interpretation, etc.—History—20th century.
I. Title.
BS2595.2P67     1990
226.4′06—dc20
                                                            89-36222
                                                                CIP

Published by Paulist Press
997 Macarthur Boulevard
Mahwah, NJ 07430

Printed and bound in the
United States of America

# Contents

Abbreviations      vii

Introduction      1

1. Luke: Historian, Theologian, Artist      5
2. The Composition of Luke's Gospel      16
3. The Concerns of Luke's Community      42
4. Christ and Salvation in the Gospel of Luke      60
5. Political and Social Issues in Luke's Gospel      82
6. Spiritual and Pastoral Concerns in the Gospel of Luke      103

Conclusions      122

Notes      125

For Further Reading      141

*In memory of my mother*
*Norma Arlene Larson Powell*
*(1924–1979)*

# Abbreviations

| | |
|---|---|
| AB | Anchor Bible |
| AnBib | Analecta Biblica |
| *ANQ* | *Andover Newton Quarterly* |
| BBB | Bonner Biblische Beiträge |
| *BTB* | *Biblical Theology Bulletin* |
| *BToday* | *Bible Today* |
| BWANT | Beiträge zur Wissenschaft vom Alten und Neuen Testament |
| *BZ* | *Biblische Zeitschrift* |
| BZNW | Beihefte zur Zeitschrift für die neutestamentliche Wissenschaft |
| *CBQ* | *Catholic Biblical Quarterly* |
| *CHSP* | *Center for Hermeneutical Studies Protocol Series* |
| *DG* | *Drew Gateway* |
| EBib | Etudes bibliques |
| EH | Europäische Hochshulschriften |
| FRLANT | Forschungen zur Religion und Literatur des Alten und Neuen Testament |
| GNS | Good News Studies |
| *JAAR* | *Journal of the American Academy of Religion* |
| *JBL* | *Journal of Biblical Literature* |

| | |
|---|---|
| JSNTSS | Journal for the Study of the New Testament Supplement Series |
| MBS | Message of Biblical Spirituality |
| NIC | New International Commentary |
| *NRT* | *La nouvelle revue théologique* |
| NTSMS | New Testament Studies Monograph Series |
| PC | Proclamation Commentaries |
| SANT | Studien zum Alten und Neuen Testament |
| SB | Stuttgarter Bibelstudien |
| *ScEsp* | *Science et esprit* |
| SNTSMS | Society for New Testament Studies Monograph Series |
| SNTU | Studien zum Neuen Testament und seiner Umwelt |
| SNTW | Studies of the New Testament and Its World |
| StNeo | Studia neotestamentica |
| SZNT | Studien zum Neuen Testament |
| *TB* | *Tyndale Bulletin* |
| TI | Theological Inquiries |
| *TJ* | *Trinity Journal* |
| *TToday* | *Theology Today* |
| *USQR* | *Union Seminary Quarterly Review* |
| *ZNW* | *Zeitschrift für die neutestamentliche Wissenschaft* |

# Introduction

One way to appreciate the impact that Luke's Gospel has had on Christianity is to try to envision what things would be like without it. Can we imagine Christmas without shepherds or a baby in a manger? Liturgy without any Magnificat, Gloria, Benedictus, or Nunc Dimmitis? A church year without Ascension or Pentecost? How many favorite Bible stories would we lose? Zacchaeus, the Prodigal Son, the Good Samaritan . . . all would be gone forever.

The French rationalist Renan called this Gospel, "the most beautiful book in the world."[1] In 1966, however, a modern scholar described the work in terms that were decidedly less sentimental. He referred to it as "a storm center" in contemporary scholarship.[2] That label has stuck. Among modern scholars, questions have arisen concerning almost every aspect of this "beautiful book": questions regarding the intentions and circumstances of its author, even questions as to the nature of the work itself.

The purpose of this book is to introduce the reader to some of these questions and to indicate trends that contemporary scholarship is taking with regard to the Gospel of Luke. By and large, the topics selected for discussion here are those receiving the most attention in current scholarly literature. At times, the reader may wonder whether these scholars are able to agree on *anything*, but this impression is partly determined by the fact that disputed matters are naturally the ones that are most discussed. The perceptive reader may also note that divergent opinions are not always mutually exclusive. Even so, there are a lot of different ideas about Luke out there, and it must be admitted that the "storm center" label is still apt.

The overall intention of this survey is to identify trends in Lukan scholarship rather than to simply review or recommend particular books. Still, the best way to examine these trends is often to look at representative samples of works that are being produced. This approach is not exhaustive, however, for in every case there are many other works that could be discussed.

The first chapter considers various methodological approaches to Luke that are used by scholars who approach the Gospel with different goals in mind. Chapter Two presents the dominant theories concerning Luke's use of sources in the composition of his Gospel. The third chapter addresses the question of why Luke wrote his Gospel in the first place: what were the needs of his own community that prompted such an undertaking? Chapter Four is devoted to what have unquestionably been the major theological issues in Lukan studies: christology, eschatology, and salvation history. The fifth chapter focuses on less traditional matters that are nevertheless receiving a great deal of attention, namely the political and social implications of this Gospel. Finally, Chapter Six considers questions related to Luke's concept of discipleship and the Christian life.

The focus of this book is on Luke's Gospel, although it is sometimes necessary to consider insights based on the study of his second work as well. It is accepted as axiomatic today that the author of our third Gospel is also the author of the book of Acts, and much of the scholarship discussed in this book bases its conclusions on references to both works. Nevertheless, there are certain issues that would be relevant to a study of Acts that do not receive adequate treatment here. In short, attention is paid to research that uses Acts as "a commentary on Luke's Gospel," but not necessarily to that which uses the Gospel as "a commentary on Acts."[3]

It is my hope that this book will prove interesting to readers who would simply like to know what scholars are saying about Luke without entering into the fray themselves. For the more serious student, on the other hand, I hope that it will also prove useful as a stimulus to further research. The arguments of all the scholars presented here are based on careful and detailed exegetical studies and it has not been possible to reproduce all the evidence for each position. The student should not, therefore, attempt to evaluate the various opinions solely on the basis of what is offered here, but is encouraged to go to the scholars themselves and examine their works in more detail. Of course, I hope that all my readers will go also to Luke and read his Gospel with new interest, new insight, and new appreciation for what (storm center or not) remains a thing of beauty.

I am grateful to Lawrence Boadt and to Paulist Press for giving me the opportunity to present this study and to Trinity Lutheran Seminary in Columbus, Ohio for providing me with a community and academic atmosphere conducive to such work. Special thanks go to Melissa Curtis for typing and correcting the manuscript.

# 1
# Luke: Historian, Theologian, Artist

The "Gospel According to Luke" is read by a wide variety of people with a diverse assortment of interests. Historians sometimes scour its pages for details about life in the Roman empire or for information regarding the situation in Palestine during the first century of the Christian era. Sociologists are fascinated by this early product of a social movement that would someday become a major world religion. Preachers find it a rich resource for homilies, and even the most secular reader appreciates its stories.

In the Christian Church, of course, the main interest in Luke concerns its role as Scripture, but it is nevertheless examined in a variety of ways: The student of Luke today is well-supplied with methodological approaches. He or she may choose from a panoply of tools: source criticism, form criticism, redaction criticism, narrative criticism, structuralism, sociological exegesis, and so on.[1] This diversity enriches the science of biblical interpretation even as it complicates it. The old texts are seldom in danger of appearing old; they are constantly being read in new and different ways.

This chapter will examine a sampling of three major approaches to Luke, namely, perspectives that regard the evangelist as a historian, as a theologian, and as a literary artist.

## Luke the Historian

Until recently, Luke's Gospel was read, together with the book of Acts, as a history of Christian origins. The two-volume work was considered a vast storehouse of information for reconstructing what happened in the lives of Jesus and his earliest followers. Modern times, however, have brought a new historical consciousness and a refinement of critical methodologies for conducting historical research. Luke the historian has fallen on hard times.[2]

There is, of course, a problem with the nature of the work itself. Can any narrative that reports, in so cavalier a fashion, the workings of fantastic miracles and the adventures of angels and demons be read today as history? But even aside from this predilection for the supernatural, Luke's competence as a historian is called into question. For example, there are several discrepancies between his account of the Jerusalem council in Acts 15 and the account given by one who was actually there in Galatians 2. Or, again, Luke's knowledge of Palestinian geography seems so inadequate at times that one prominent scholar was led to remark, "Jesus' route cannot be reconstructed on any map and, in any case, Luke did not possess one."[3]

Furthermore, it is doubtful whether the writing of history was ever Luke's intent. Luke wrote to proclaim, to persuade, and to interpret; he did not write to preserve records for posterity. An awareness of this has been, for many, the final nail in Luke the historian's coffin. If Luke intended to write history, he did so poorly, but he did not so intend. Luke is a theologian, not a historian.

One scholar who is not happy with this dichotomy is I. H. Marshall. The title of his book *Luke: Historian and Theologian* gives away his position.[4] Luke is a theologian, Marshall agrees, but he is also a historian. His interest, admittedly, is not simply in recording history for its own sake, but in interpreting its significance for salvation. At the same time, however, he is careful not to misrepresent facts or to fabricate history in the interests of his theology.

According to Marshall, it is Luke's view of theology that leads him to write history. For Luke, faith must be rooted in history, even though it involves more than mere acceptance of historical facts. For example, a central statement of faith for Luke would be, "God raised Jesus from the dead" (Acts 2:32; 3:15, 22; 4:10; 10:40; 13:30). There are two elements here, the historical fact that Jesus rose from the dead and the theological interpretation that this was an act of God. If the event of the resurrection was not historical, then for Luke, theological reflection on it would be impossible and faith would be reduced to obstinate and irrational fantasy. For Luke, the historical basis of the resurrection is significant (Acts 1:3, 22).

Because Luke does not want to falsify faith, Marshall believes, he is driven to become a historian. In the prologue of his Gospel, he emphasizes the accuracy of what is presented, giving his own credentials as one who has "followed all things closely" (1:3), stressing the reliability of his sources, some of whom are "eyewitnesses" (1:2), and stating his intent to present things "accurately" and "in order" (1:3–4). All this indicates that Luke does intend to be taken seriously as a historian.

Marshall also believes that modern skeptics have been too hasty in their assessment of Luke's abilities. The apparent discrepancies concerning the Jerusalem council, for instance, can be resolved if the account in Galatians is read as referring to a different, earlier meeting. Similarly, many of the so-called geographical inaccuracies stem from a failure to recognize that Luke uses terms differently than we do today. He uses "Judea" in a narrow sense to refer to the particular region, but also in a broader sense to refer to all of Palestine.

In short, Marshall thinks that interest in Luke as a historian should be revived and his reputation as such rehabilitated.

## Luke the Theologian

Whatever value Luke's writings may have as history, most scholars today are more interested in the contribution they make to theology. Luke is viewed as a very capable and original theologian, whose interpretation of early traditions played a major role in the development of Christianity.

One of the first to study Luke from this perspective was Hans Conzelmann. His book *Die Mitte der Zeit* is available in an English translation called *The Theology of St. Luke.*[5] As a pioneer in redaction criticism, Conzelmann studies the way Luke edits his source material. Luke is not a disinterested compiler, he concludes, but an innovator, who reworks tradition according to a set theological agenda.

The overriding theological concept that emerges from Conzelmann's study is Luke's scheme of salvation history. Luke divides all of time, from creation to the end of the world, into three epochs: 1) the time of Israel, 2) the time of Jesus' earthly ministry, and 3) the time of the Church.

As simple as this scheme appears, it has far-reaching theological implications. For one thing, it assumes a significant interim between the time of Jesus' earthly ministry and the end of the world. From Paul's epistles and the Gospel of Mark, it is apparent that early Christians lived in imminent expectation of Jesus' return. Luke, however, allows for a delay and thus the parousia loses its significance as a key factor in Christian hope and as a decisive motive for Christian living.

In addition, Conzelmann claims that Luke has "historicized" the message and ministry of Jesus. Since Luke and his community live during the "time of the Church," they are able to look back on the events of Jesus' life as belonging to a past epoch, different from their own. This is why Luke portrays Jesus as giving instructions to his disciples (9:3) that will no longer apply in the days to come (22:35–36).

In short, Luke shifts the emphasis in Christian faith from the future to the past. By his description of past events, however, he intends to instruct the Church of his own day. He is interested in the Church as an institution within world history, a matter that did not concern Jesus or his earliest followers. This is why he plays down the role of the Roman empire in his account of Jesus' death (23:4, 14, 20–23) and attempts to show that Jesus was politically harmless (20:21–25). He believes that if the Church is to endure, it must make peace with the world and learn to coexist with society.

The question of continuity, of course, is an important one and Conzelmann believes that Luke has given it much thought. By emphasizing the idea of promise and fulfillment, he establishes Jesus' relationship to the time of Israel before him. Similarly, the motifs of apostolic tradition and the gift of the Holy Spirit assure continuity between the past time of Jesus and the current era of the Church. Because the Church proclaims the message concerning Jesus, based on apostolic tradition, it becomes the guardian of tradition and the channel of salvation in the present age. The gift of the Holy Spirit is reinterpreted by Luke to become, not a sign that the Kingdom has come, but a guarantee that it will come and a "provisional substitute" for the parousia that makes it possible to live in the interim.

Conzelmann's treatment of Luke's theology has been the starting point for many discussions in recent years. As will become evident in the next few chapters of this book, however, scholars have taken issue with practically every point that Conzelmann makes. One notable critic has observed that widespread agreement on anything in Luke is difficult to find, "except on the point that Conzelmann's synthesis is inadequate."[6]

There is consensus on another point as well. Even if they disagree on the particulars of Luke's theology, scholars would not argue with Conzelmann's identification of him as a theologian. Today, the third evangelist is universally recognized as "a theologian of no mean stature who very consciously and deliberately planned and executed his work."[7]

## Luke the Artist

At some point in church history, a legend arose that Luke was a skilled painter and, to this day, there is at least one cathedral in Spain that claims to have a portrait of the Madonna executed by him. This is not, however, what scholars mean when they say that Luke is an artist. The reference, rather, is to his literary art, his skill in composing a narrative.

In recent years there has been increasing interest in the Gospels as narratives.[8] This approach goes beyond the "redaction criticism" practiced by Hans Conzelmann in that it views the evangelist as an author in his own right, rather than as simply an editor who worked with various sources. As a result, the focus of literary criticism is on the unity of the work in its final form instead of on the layers of tradition that lie behind it.

In accord with this new approach, a veteran Lukan scholar, Robert Karris, has written a book called *Luke: Artist and Theologian* that treats Luke's passion account as literature.[9] Karris views Luke's Gospel as a "kerygmatic story," that is, as a story that intends to proclaim the good news about Jesus and the rule of God.[10] He finds the work replete with "themes" that the author artistically develops throughout the narrative. These include, for example, the themes of "faithfulness," "justice," and "food."[11] Karris is more interested in elucidating the meaning of Luke's kerygmatic story than in reconstructing the historical events that lie behind it. He is also more interested in seeing themes that are important to the work as a whole than he is in isolating particular units of tradition and interpreting them in light of their compositional history.

The most comprehensive study of Luke from this perspective is Robert Tannehill's *The Narrative Unity of Luke-Acts: A Literary Interpretation*.[12] Tannehill reads Luke's story as more than a string of episodes. The work has a unified plot, as can be seen by its internal connections, developed character roles, and unifying purpose.

The internal connections consist of literary "echoes and reminders" that relate various parts of the narrative to each other. For example, John the Baptist warns against substituting an appeal to Abraham for repentance (3:8), but, in an entirely different part of the Gospel, a rich man does exactly that (16:24, 27, 30). Luke's story is replete with touches like this that serve as "an internal commentary on the story, clarifying meanings and suggesting additional nuances."[13] In addition, the Gospel is characterized by an abundance of "previews and reviews," statements that direct the reader ahead to what is going to happen (e.g., 9:22, 44; 18:31–33; 22:21; 31–34) or back to reconsider what has already occurred (e.g., 24:7, 25–26, 44, 46). The narrative is held together by distinctive themes, which are sometimes developed, dropped, and then picked up again later in the story. For example, Luke tells three stories about Jesus eating with tax collectors and sinners (5:29–32; 15:1–32; 19:1–10) and three stories about him healing on the sabbath (6:6–11; 13:10–17; 14:1–6). These recurrent "type scenes" are repetitious but also demonstrate a variety that provides richer development of the theme while unifying the narrative.

Tannehill's literary analysis of Luke also focuses on the major roles of characters who interact within the narrative. He finds that, like any good author, Luke presents and develops his characters with consistency and purpose. Jesus, the main character, is represented as one who is powerful in word and deed (24:19; Acts 1:1), but also as one who must come to an understanding of his mission through a process of development (1:80; 2:40, 52). After the Spirit comes upon him and a voice declares that he is God's Son (3:22), he must overcome false conceptions of what it means to be the Son of God (4:1–13). Only then can he declare with confidence why the Spirit has come upon him: to preach good news to the poor and to proclaim release to captives (4:16–21). Throughout the rest of the narrative, Jesus' authoritative teaching and mighty acts demonstrate the fulfillment of this commission. God is at work in Jesus to fulfill a comprehensive hope for Israel and the world.

Other characters in the story are interesting because of their interactions with Jesus. The religious authorities, for instance, serve as examples of what Luke does *not* want his readers to be. They are rich and greedy (16:14), they are hypocritical (12:1) and self-righteous (16:15; 18:9–14), and they reject God's purpose for themselves (7:30). In the story, however, their most important role is as the opponents of Jesus, as obstacles who would stand in the way of his divine mission (5:31–32) and as recalcitrants whose rejection of him threatens to thwart God's great plan.

The disciples, on the other hand, provide a positive example of detachment from possessions when they "leave all" to follow Jesus (5:11, 28; 18:28). There are tensions, however, between Jesus and his disciples also. The latter are insightful (9:20) and powerful (9:6; 10:17) in many ways, but because they are unable to understand the necessity of Jesus' suffering and rejection (9:45; 18:34), they are also failures in important respects. They entertain premature messianic expectations (17:22; 19:11; Acts 1:6) and, failing to accept rejection and suffering as a necessary part of their own discipleship, they engage in petty rivalries over rank (9:46, 22:24) and become apostate in the face of death (22:54–66). They must witness Jesus' death (23:49) and resurrection (24:34–49; Acts 1:22) before they can understand how suffering and rejection fit into the plan of God.

More than anything else, it is Luke's concept of divine purpose that makes his two-volume work a "narrative unity." The purpose of God, which stands behind all of the events that are narrated, is disclosed at key points throughout the story. Angelic announcements (1:13–17, 30–37; 2:10–14), prophetic predictions (1:46–55, 67–74; 2:29–35, 38) and quotations from Scripture (3:4–6; 4:18–19) all point to the same thing: universal salvation. It is amazing, however, that this purpose is not completely fulfilled. As Luke tells the story, the joyous recognition that God has visited God's people (1:68, 78) gives way to a mournful realization that God's people do not know the time of their visitation (19:44). In a sense, then, the story Luke tells is a tragedy. The great purpose of God is rejected (7:30) and the hope that Jesus would redeem Israel (24:21) apparently goes unfulfilled.

The story, however, is not completely tragic. Ultimately, it reveals that God can even use human opposition to further the divine purpose. In the book of Acts, it becomes apparent that Israel's rejection of Jesus has become the occasion for the mission to the Gentiles. The purpose of ultimate salvation is not abandoned, though even at the end of the second volume, the tension within the plot is unresolved. Thus, the story emerges as "a dialogue between God and a recalcitrant humanity." As such, it is all the more relevant to readers whose life-experience includes rejection and defeat as well as success.[14]

## Observations and Conclusions

In the remaining chapters of this book it will become obvious that scholars have come to different conclusions regarding the Gospel of Luke. This chapter indicates that one reason for this is that they sometimes begin by asking different sorts of questions.

There are, however, points of common concern. One issue raised by all the scholars discussed in this chapter is the extent of Luke's originality. I. H. Marshall views Luke as a conservative editor who is working mostly with traditional material. He is not an innovator but a careful historian whose views may therefore be understood as consistent with the message of Jesus. Hans Conzelmann distinguishes much more sharply between the "kerygma" or content of early Christian proclamation and the distinctive theological stamp that Luke has placed upon it. He does this by constantly comparing Luke with his source material and indicating significant and consistent alterations the evangelist has made. Robert Tannehill finds that

Luke's originality goes way beyond simple editorial changes and extends to his composition of the narrative as a whole. Questions regarding Luke's method of composition and use of source material will be discussed more fully in the next chapter.

Another question arises from this: If Luke is innovative and original in his theological contributions, how is this to be evaluated? In the wake of Hans Conzelmann's work, Luke's theology has often been viewed negatively, as a falling away from the essence of primitive Christianity.[15] Scholars have sometimes called Luke "early Catholic," a term that is used with some ambiguity but that is generally not meant as a compliment. Luke identifies the gospel with Christianity, presents Jesus as the founder of a religion, and portrays the Church as an ordered institution that dispenses salvation.[16] The extent to which Luke does this, of course, is argued, as is the question of whether it is a bad thing.[17] Ernst Käsemann exemplifies this difficulty in evaluating Luke when he calls him "the greatest New Testament theologian," but admits "the price he must pay" to be this is "by no means small."[18]

Finally, though it is appropriate today to think of Luke as a historian, theologian, and literary artist, it must be noted that the middle term predominates. As the titles of the books by Marshall and Karris indicate, no one is saying that Luke is *not* a theologian; the argument is simply that a full consideration of his work should include other dimensions as well. Similarly, Tannehill does not imagine that Luke has written his story for literary reasons alone; rather, he uses narrative as a form of theological expression. That Luke "does theology" no one will doubt; how he does it, and how it is to be evaluated are questions that continue to evoke discussion.

# 2
# The Composition of Luke's Gospel

Luke's Gospel is anonymous. It begins with a prologue that specifies a particular recipient (1:3), but the author does not identify himself or name the sources he claims to have used. Perhaps he just assumed his intended readers would know this information, or perhaps he thought it didn't matter. In any case, his book is anonymous.

Scholars, however, have not been content to leave the matter at that. The attempt to identify the author of this work and the sources that he used has occupied students of the Bible for centuries. Today, there are many who believe a satisfactory resolution has been found, while, for others, the quest goes on.

## Authorship

Church tradition attributes the third Gospel to "Luke the physician, a companion of Paul" (cf. Col 4:14; 2 Tim 4:11; Phlm 24). Since the derivation of this tradition is uncertain,[1] it is difficult to evaluate. Still, traditions must come from somewhere, and it is often asked why anyone would invent such a story if it were not true. Would they not rather attribute the work to someone more noteworthy?

Some scholars find support for this tradition in certain passages of Acts, where the author uses the pronoun "we"

16

(16:10–17; 20:5–15; 21:1–18; 27:1–28:16). They believe that this indicates he is present with Paul in those instances. Others have suggested that this is only a literary device or a carry-over from a source that the evangelist might have used.[2]

The greatest argument against the tradition has been the claim that this author shows no knowledge of Paul's epistles, little understanding of his theology, and only slight appreciation for his main concerns (e.g., justification by grace, freedom from the law, and his own apostleship).[3] Even if these observations are correct, however, they are not conclusive. There is no reason a companion of Paul's could not have been an independent thinker.

Because pseudepigraphy was widely practiced in the New Testament era and the tendency to link favored writings with an established name was pronounced, scholars are usually skeptical of traditions regarding authorship. Very few, for example, identify the author of the Gospel of Matthew as one of Jesus' twelve disciples. With regard to Luke, however, there may be a trend toward cautious acceptance. A survey of recent commentaries reveals that many are willing to accept the author of this Gospel as a companion of Paul so long as he is not regarded as the latter's disciple.[4] And for those who can accept the author as one of Paul's associates, "Luke the physician" seems as likely a candidate as any.[5]

## Luke's Use of Mark

Luke begins his Gospel with the statement that many others have undertaken to compile narratives similar to his (1:1). Although he does not say who these "many" were, scholars generally assume that one of the works he refers to is the Gospel of Mark. Comparative analysis reveals that three large blocks of Luke's Gospel (3:1–6:19; 8:4–9:50; 18:15–24:11) are comprised mainly of material that is also found in Mark. Furthermore, the material contained in these three blocks is usually reported in the same narrative order as it is in Mark.

It makes sense to many, then, to view Luke's Gospel as a combination of material from Mark with other material. There are two different views as to how such a combination took place. The first is that the evangelist inserted the three blocks of material from Mark into an already-formed earlier version of his Gospel, sometimes called "Proto-Luke."[6] The second view is that the evangelist started with Mark and then expanded it by inserting new material (6:20–8:3; 9:51–18:14) and adding the infancy narratives and resurrection stories to the beginning and end.[7]

In either case, the material from Mark is not simply transmitted word for word. The evangelist modifies what he takes over from Mark and makes it his own. In the introduction to his Anchor Bible commentary, Joseph Fitzmyer lists some of the ways in which Luke edits his source material.[8] For one thing, he frequently improves the Greek style and language. He changes the historic present tense to the more precise past tense and he eliminates superfluous pronouns. He introduces features of more literary Greek, such as the optative mood, and he greatly increases use of the genitive absolute. Luke also avoids Aramaic expressions, such as the "Talitha cumi" of Mark 5:41 (cf. Lk 8:54). Changes such as this suggest that Luke's community may have been composed mostly of Gentiles, including some who could appreciate the higher class of Greek.

Other changes are due to Luke's overall literary scheme. Since he chooses to orient his story of Jesus toward Jerusalem, he often omits other geographical references, or even whole episodes that place the focus elsewhere. Jesus does not, for example, predict a post-resurrection reunion with his disciples in Galilee (Mk 14:28). Luke also transposes Markan material for literary purposes. He moves the story of Jesus' rejection at Nazareth (Mk 6:1–6) up to the very beginning of his Galilean ministry (4:16–30) so that it can serve as a programmatic introduction to all that follows. Similarly, he moves Mark's report about the crowds who followed Jesus (3:7–12; cf. Lk 6:12–16) up a few verses to provide a logical audience for the sermon he wants to insert (6:20–49). These transpositions are exceptions to the general observation that Luke follows Mark's narrative order in his presentation of episodes. In all, Fitzmyer finds seven such exceptions, all of which may be explained for literary reasons.[9]

Luke often abbreviates Mark's stories by omitting what he considers to be insignificant or inappropriate. Apparently, he does not find Mark's note regarding the incompetence of physicians (5:26) particularly relevant to the story of the woman with a hemorrhage (Lk 8:42–48). In his account of the epileptic demoniac (9:37–43), he fails to include the extended conversation between Jesus and the boy's father (cf. Mk 9:21–24). Sometimes he may pass over material in order to avoid a "doublet," or duplication of a story he has in another form. He eliminates Mark's account of the anointing at Bethany (14:3–9) but includes elsewhere a very different anointing story (Lk 7:36–50).

Fitzmyer detects a "delicate sensitivity" in Luke that leads him to avoid anything that smacks of the violent, the passionate, or the emotional. The overturning of tables in the Temple (Mk 11:15–16) and the crowning of Jesus with thorns (Mk 15:16–20) are both eliminated, as is the highly-charged story of Herodias and John the Baptist (Mk 6:14–29). References to Jesus' emotions are also omitted. Mark's descriptions of Jesus as stern (1:43), angry (3:5; 10:14), distressed (14:33–34) and sad (3:5) seem inappropriate to Luke, but not just because they are "negative" emotions. Luke also omits references to Jesus feeling compassion (Mk 1:41) and love (Mk 10:21). Fitzmyer suggests that, for this evangelist, the attribution of any human emotion to Jesus detracted in some way from his nobility.

Luke's concern to enhance the image of Jesus also carries over to such figures as the disciples and Jesus' family. He does not include, for example, Mark's comment that Jesus' relatives thought he was "beside himself" (3:21). Similarly, the stories of Jesus rebuking Peter (Mk 8:33), of James and John's presumptuous request (Mk 10:35–40), and of the disciples' flight at Jesus' arrest (Mk 14:49) are found nowhere in Luke.

Fitzmyer is representative of most Lukan scholars in finding a variety of reasons, some literary and some theological, to explain Luke's work as a redactor. Of course, his particular explanations are open to question: some would say that Luke has no aversion to recounting doublets (cf. 13:10–17; 14:1–6) or describing violence (Acts 1:18; 12:20–23). The basic methodology, however, is well-established. A great many scholars begin their study of Luke by comparing his Gospel to that of Mark, noting what has been changed, and asking, "why?"

In the long run, though, it is not as simple as that, for there are other questions to take into consideration. For one thing, it must be asked to what extent Luke's differences from Mark reflect his own perspective. Tim Schramm, in a German study called *Der Markus-Stoff bei Lukas* (i.e., The Markan Material in Luke), warns against attributing modifications to Luke that may actually derive from one of his other sources.[10] For example, many interpreters are quick to note Luke's addition of 5:39 to the sayings he takes over from Mark in 5:33–38 (cf. Mk 2:18–22).

Thus, Jesus now concludes his sayings about new wine in old wineskins by adding, "No one after drinking old wine desires new, for he says, 'The old is good.'" This addition, it is claimed, represents Luke's own interpretation of the preceding verses and casts the original tradition in a very different light. Schramm, however, regards the verse as a miscellaneous saying that Luke had among his sources. It is placed here simply on the basis of word association. It is not intended to explain the Markan passage and, in any case, it is no more original with Luke than the other verses. According to a set of linguistic criteria he develops, Schramm identifies almost half of all Luke's modifications of Mark as attributable to his other sources. Nevertheless, most modern scholars believe Luke's intentions can be seen in his juxtaposition of traditional materials as well as in his own, more direct contributions.

Another question scholars must consider when they examine Luke's use of Mark is the status of the evangelist's Markan text. In Lukan studies, Mark 6:45–8:26 is sometimes called "the big omission" and Mark 9:41–10:12 "the little omission," because Luke does not include any material from these sections. Unable to explain such lapses, some interpreters have proposed that Luke's copy of Mark was defective or incomplete. To most, though, it appears that he intentionally skips the material. Fitzmyer, for instance, explains the big omission as a desire to avoid the change in geographical focus.

These types of questions have required redaction critics to pay careful attention to linguistic and textual matters, but, in the final analysis, have not stymied their research. A potentially more devastating challenge is posed by those who question whether Luke made use of Mark at all. This objection will be discussed below, but first it is necessary to consider another matter.

## Luke's Use of Q

The Gospel of Mark may have been one of the "many" sources Luke claims to have used (1:1), but what were the others? Many parallels can also be found with the Gospel of Matthew. Did he use this book as well? For various reasons, most scholars do not think this was the case. Rather, the proposal is that Matthew and Luke both used another source, which is now lost to us. This source, for reasons that are also lost, is known as "Q."[11]

John Kloppenborg attempts to describe this lost source in his book, *The Formation of Q.*[12] He regards it as a written document that was probably composed in Greek. It was primarily a collection of sayings with very little narrative, not even an account of Jesus' passion. The order of the sayings, which is best preserved in Luke, reveals that they were grouped topically and in accord with certain unifying motifs. Although it is possible that some portions of Q may have been omitted by both evangelists or may be reflected only in the *Sondergut* (unique material) of Luke or Matthew, Kloppenborg believes the bulk of the document is preserved in the "double tradition," that is, in the material that is found in both Luke and Matthew but not in Mark. The amount of overlap between Q and Mark also appears to have been slight. The formative component of Q was six "wisdom speeches" of Jesus that called for a new orientation of life in light of God's coming Kingdom. To these were added some polemical materials intended to demonstrate that the matters over which Jesus was reproached by Israel were virtues rather than causes for shame. Finally, the temptation story (Mt 4:1–11; Lk 4:1–13) was added as a preface to show that Jesus himself conformed to the ethic that he advocated. The addition of this pericope was a step toward the more biographical character of the Gospels.

Another Q scholar, Richard Edwards, has asked what sort of Christian community could have produced such a document.[13] In *A Theology of Q*, Edwards notes that three kinds of sayings are interwoven in the Q tradition: wisdom, prophetic, and eschatological. The function of the sayings is, first, to proclaim the dawning of God's Kingdom and the imminent return of Jesus as the Son of Man. In addition, they describe in a very practical way what is required of those who will survive the judgment. For this community, there is neither time nor need to speculate on the meaning of Jesus' death. Discipleship is their primary interest. They have collected the sayings of their coming Judge to serve as a guide for living in the last days. Indeed, Edwards follows Heinz Tödt in believing the Q community conceived of its task as continuing to speak the words of Jesus rather than as preaching about him.[14] This task was fulfilled not only by collecting and repeating his sayings, but also by allowing inspired prophets to speak through his name.

Though such reconstructions are intriguing, many Lukan scholars are ultimately more interested in how the evangelist incorporates the Q material into his Gospel. With a few exceptions, these passages occur in two blocks of the Gospel that also contain material peculiar to Luke (6:20–8:3; 9:51–18:14). These blocks are sometimes called the "little interpolation" (6:20–8:3) and the "big interpolation" (9:51–18:14) because they interrupt the flow of material taken mainly from Mark (3:1–6:19; 8:4–9:50; 18:15–24:11).

The little interpolation is best known for its account of Jesus' Sermon on the Plain (6:20–49). These verses derive from Q and are often compared to Matthew's longer and more developed Sermon on the Mount (Mt 5:1–7:27). A study of these two sermons by Jan Lambrecht attempts to explain how each of the evangelists makes use of the Q material.[15] Although Luke's version is shorter, Lambrecht does not believe he omits anything from Q; rather, it is Matthew who makes significant additions. Luke does, however, alter his source in other ways. With regard to the beatitudes (6:20–26), for instance, three changes are significant. First, Luke rewords the beatitudes in the second person in order to emphasize their application to his readers. Second, he introduces a temporal distinction not present in the original by adding the word "now" at key points (6:21). Instead of simply proclaiming the paradoxical blessedness of those who appear wretched, Jesus is now represented as contrasting present wretchedness with future glory. Finally, Luke introduces an element of threat by adding the "woe passages" (6:24–26), which reverse the situations described in the beatitudes. Significantly, these woe passages are also worded in the second person and they also turn on the temporal distinction marked by the word "now" (6:25). This time, however, the message is that those who enjoy good things now will be deprived in the life to come (6:24–26).

The effect of Luke's redaction is to transform what was originally *proclamation* of the Kingdom into *instruction* concerning this life and the next. The latter element was not entirely absent from Q, but in Luke it comes to the fore. The content of that instruction also shows Lukan development insofar as it predicts an eventual reversal of fortune. In Q, Jesus simply proclaimed that God favors the poor (including persecuted Christians) and will right their cause shortly. In Luke, he addresses both poor and rich Christians, informing them that their current status will be reversed in the life to come. This theme is present elsewhere in Luke (e.g., 16:19–31) and may be behind another change he makes later in this sermon: Christians who are able should "lend" money to people who cannot pay them back. If they do, their reward in heaven will be great (6:34–

35). These verses were not present in the original Q. Like the woe passages, they were added by Luke. It can be seen, then, that Luke treats this sermon from Q not as an eschatological proclamation of the Kingdom but as instruction for the present day. He also develops that instruction in keeping with one of his favorite themes, the need for the redistribution of wealth.

Aside from the Sermon on the Plain and some other parts of the "little interpolation" (6:8–8:3), most of Luke's Q material can be found in the "big interpolation" of 9:51–18:14. Here, it is once again woven together with other material in what appears to be a conscious composition of the evangelist. This section is of special interest to scholars because it forms the bulk of what has been called "Luke's Travel Narrative" (9:51–19:48).[16]

In his study, *Jesus' Mission to Jerusalem*, Helmuth Egelkraut emphasizes the importance of this section for understanding the Gospel of Luke.[17] It comprises at least one-third of the total work and is organized around a theme that is especially important to Luke. That theme is the journey of Jesus to Jerusalem. At the very beginning of this section, Luke tells us that Jesus "set his face to go to Jerusalem" (9:51) and over the next ten chapters we are repeatedly reminded that he is still on his way there.[18] It is unlikely, however, that this is a historical record of Jesus' actual travels. The itinerary Luke describes seems artificial since, as one scholar observes, Jesus is traveling to Jerusalem the entire time but never seems to make any progress.[19] At times, he seems to be drawing near and then, inexplicably, he is suddenly farther away. Furthermore, most of the material in this section bears no necessary or immediate connection to the journey theme. The Q material, for instance, is found in completely different contexts in Matthew, contexts that have nothing to do with a journey to

Jerusalem. The journey, then, should be regarded as a framework that Luke has created for this section of his Gospel. It sets the Q material into a narrative context that it did not possess before and it integrates it with material drawn from other sources.

Some scholars have been content to simply view the travel narrative as Luke's repository for surplus traditions, but others see it as a literary device with deliberate theological intent. One theory, for instance, is that the journey emphasizes Jesus' awareness that he must suffer. By presenting the bulk of Jesus' teachings and actions as instruction on the way to the cross, Luke imbues this material with a passion consciousness not present in the original sources.[20] Another suggestion is that the journey symbolizes discipleship, in the sense that every Christian is called to follow Jesus through suffering to glory.[21] Egelkraut, however, finds the emphasis elsewhere. He notes that Luke, as compared to his sources, enhances the polemical content of the material presented here. Most of the Q passages that are found in Luke's travel narrative occur in settings that involve conflict, although this is not true of their Matthean parallels. For example, Jesus offers the parable of the lost sheep as instruction for the Church in Matthew's Gospel (18:12–14), but in Luke it is told as a response to opposition (15:1–7). Egelkraut also notes that Jesus' conflicts are always with Israel and its leaders in this section of the Gospel, rather than with his own disciples.

Accordingly, Egelkraut surmises that the theological purpose of the travel narrative is to explain God's judgment on Israel and Jerusalem. Jesus' journey is emblematic of God's visitation, a visitation that is resisted and finally rejected. This journey, or, rather, visitation, is intensely eschatological because, for Israel, the kingdom is present and the crisis imminent. Jesus urgently calls upon his Jewish opponents to recognize this, but by rejecting him they forfeit their only chance of avoiding judgment. Even as he conducts his mission to Jerusalem, however, Jesus is gathering about him a community of religious outcasts who will serve as the matrix for the new people of God. In the travel narrative, then, Luke records how Israel rejects the kingdom and how, consequently, Israel's place in God's economy is taken by others. This lesson was not in the Q material itself, but, by placing that material in conflict settings and making it a part of Jesus' journey to Jerusalem, Luke interprets Q according to his own theological perspective.

The goal of these studies by Lambrecht and Egelkraut is to interpret Luke's intentions and emphases by noting modifications he has made in the Q source. This, of course, is the same goal pursued by those who study Luke's use of Mark, but with regard to Q the matter is more complex. When Luke's material differs from its Matthean parallel, it must be asked which of the evangelists preserves the original Q version and which has made the changes. How do scholars make such assessments? One way to proceed is to consider the potential motivation that either evangelist might have had for editing the source material and then determine which of the proposed redactions seems the most likely. In addition, it is usually assumed that both Matthew and Luke would have edited Q according to the same principles they followed in editing Mark. Guidelines for understanding their treatment of the source that has been lost to us, then, can be discerned by observing their treatment of the one we do possess.

There are some scholars, however, who have problems with the basic assumptions of this approach. It is to these that we now turn our attention.

**Challenges to the Two-Source Hypothesis**

The view that both Matthew and Luke made use of Mark and the now-lost Q source in the composition of their Gospels is called the "Two-Source Hypothesis." Although this theory is espoused by the majority of New Testament scholars today, the literary relationship of the first three Gospels has also been explained in other ways.

In his book, *The Synoptic Problem*, and in numerous other publications, William Farmer has laid the groundwork for what has come to be known as "The Two-Gospel Hypothesis."[22] This view is essentially a revival of a theory proposed by an eighteenth-century scholar, Johann Griesbach. Farmer believes, as did Griesbach, that Luke used Matthew's Gospel as a source and that Mark produced his work last, as an abridgment of Matthew and Luke. This theory, Farmer contends, adequately explains the literary agreements between these Gospels without having to posit the existence of a hypothetical "Q source" for which no material evidence exists. It also explains some things that cannot be accounted for on the basis of the Two-Source Hypothesis, such as agreements between Matthew and Luke against Mark.

But if the Two-Gospel Hypothesis solves some problems, it creates many more. In regard to the Gospel of Luke, Farmer must now account for what, to many, seems a bizarre redaction of Matthew. Why would Luke replace Matthew's infancy narrative (Mt 1:18–2:23) with a completely different version of his own (Lk 1–2)? Why would he substitute a different genealogy (Mt 1:1–17/Lk 3:23–38)? Why would he break up Matthew's great speeches of Jesus, including the Sermon on the Mount, and disperse their contents throughout his Gospel? In a now famous quotation, a New Testament scholar once said the theory that

Luke has edited Matthew in such a way would make sense only if "we had reason to believe he was a crank."[23] But Farmer believes all these changes can be understood in terms of the different literary and theological intentions of the two works. Luke is more interested than Matthew in composing a book that will meet the standards of Hellenistic historiography. Whereas Matthew reports the coming of Jesus in terms that relate primarily to Israel, Luke sets his infancy account (and genealogy) against a background of world history. In addition, Luke moves much of Jesus' teaching to the central portion of his Gospel where it is framed and interpreted by material peculiar to him, namely the several parables that emphasize God's grace and saving love (10:30–37; 15:3–32; 18:9–14). In short, Luke's redaction of Matthew can be understood in terms of his different sociological and theological orientation. Luke stands in a Rome-oriented Pauline tradition rather than in the Jerusalem-oriented Petrine tradition of Matthew.[24]

Another group of scholars, led by M. D. Goulder[25] and John Drury,[26] have also denied the existence of any so-called Q source, but they have built their argument independently of that of Farmer. They do not question, as he does, the notion that Luke used Mark as a source, but they do think that Luke's parallels with Matthew can be accounted for by a direct dependence on that Gospel. They have explained Luke's seemingly incredible editing of Matthew in terms of lectionary needs and contemporary literary practices. For example, Goulder suggests that Luke feels no compulsion to preserve the five great speeches of Jesus in Matthew because these were intended to be read on Jewish holidays no longer celebrated by Luke's congregation. Therefore, Luke breaks up the speeches and disperses their contents throughout his travel narrative, which, in his lectionary, serves as a counterpart to readings from Deuteronomy. Building on Goulder (and on C. F. Evans[27]), Drury tries to show that the entire travel narrative has been modeled on Deuteronomy. The technique used is that of "midrash," a Jewish practice of imaginatively retelling Scripture for the purpose of homiletical interpretation. Goulder and Drury believe Luke produced his Gospel as a midrash on Matthew and Mark, with frequent reference to the Old Testament. On these grounds, Luke's redaction of Matthew is explicable and Q becomes unnecessary.

If any of these challenges to the Two-Source Hypothesis could be shown to be correct, the implications for Lukan scholarship would be profound. In the first place, efforts to recover the lost Q source would be exposed as "a wild goose chase."[28] At the same time, it would become evident that the methodological basis for most recent study of Lukan theology is founded on false presuppositions. The great majority of New Testament scholars, however, have found these theories unconvincing. Still, the alternatives to the Two-Source Hypothesis have attracted a small but respectable cadre of supporters who cannot simply be ignored. One important scholar, who does in fact hold to the Two-Source Hypothesis, has stated the quandary scholars now face in basing their arguments on this proposition: "It may very well be legitimate to do so," he writes, "but so many have problems with the procedure that such an assumption narrows considerably the circles with whom one can converse."[29]

Is there any way around this impasse? Richard Edwards suggests that redaction criticism, which seeks to discover the theology of the evangelists, should properly have two parts.[30] The first part, which he calls "emendation analysis," concerns the observation of changes a redactor makes in the source material itself. This type of study is possible only to the extent that the sources can be identified. Another aspect of redaction criticism, however, is what may be called "composition analysis." This approach attempts to discern an evangelist's theological interests by noting how individual units of tradition have been ordered and arranged in the work as a whole. The emphasis is on the structure of the Gospel in question and on its recurrent literary features and patterns rather than on specific alterations that have supposedly been made in a given text. This has long been the preferred method for studying Mark and Acts,[31] since most scholars do not believe we possess any of the sources for these works. Composition criticism came to be applied to the study of Matthew's Gospel through the pioneering work of Jack Dean Kingsbury[32] and, more recently, has been applied to Luke by scholars like Joseph Tyson.[33] William Farmer agrees that the use of composition criticism holds promise for the present, during what he considers to be an interim period in which scholarly consensus regarding the sources of the Gospels is lacking.[34]

It should also be mentioned that new literary and sociological approaches to the Gospels offer methods of study that are not indentured to any particular theory of sources. For example, the analysis of Luke by Robert Tannehill that was discussed in the last chapter studies the final form of the Gospel as a narrative in its own right, without reference to earlier source material. Along with composition criticism, the new methodologies provide checks and balances on the traditional analysis of emendations. If a scholar's examination of Luke's theology as construed from a proposed redaction of sources is sound, then it should concur with studies of his theology conducted with other methods.

## Luke's Special Material

No matter what theory is espoused to explain Luke's parallels with Mark and Matthew, it can be seen that approximately one-third of his Gospel is comprised of material that is peculiar to him. Where did Luke get this material and what role does it play in his work as a whole? We will examine three types of "special material" that have, perhaps, evoked the most comment.

1) *The Infancy Narrative.* The first two chapters of Luke's Gospel are not only without parallel in the rest of the New Testament, but they are somewhat unique even within Luke's own work. Scholars have long noted the unusual style that sets these chapters apart from the rest of Luke. The infancy account is written in Greek that more closely resembles that of the Septuagint, and, as in the Old Testament, the narrative is frequently interrupted by the insertion of hymns. Even theological distinctions can be made between this section of the Gospel and the rest of Luke's work. For example, in the infancy narrative, it is said that John the Baptist will go out "in the spirit and power of Elijah" (1:17), but in the rest of the Gospel, it is Jesus, not John, who is likened to Elijah. Again, in the first two chapters, the coming of John and Jesus seems to be heralded as a sign that God is going to deliver the nation of Israel from its political oppression (1:73), but this hope is not sustained or fulfilled in the rest of the Gospel. Noting that Luke 3:1 reads like the beginning of a work, advocates of proto-Luke theories have sometimes suggested that Luke's first two chapters were not part of his original work; rather, they were attached to the front of an already-completed earlier edition, almost as an afterthought. Hans Conzelmann, in fact, did not even take these chapters into consideration when describing the theology of Luke,[35] a factor that has been almost unanimously recognized as a flaw in his work.

One of the most important studies on Luke's infancy narrative so far is that of Raymond Brown.[36] In his book, *The Birth of the Messiah*, Brown admits that if these two chapters had been lost, we would never have expected they existed. It is possible, then, that the chapters were prefixed to the rest of the Gospel as a prologue, but Brown believes Luke is nevertheless responsible for them. It is even likely that, with the exception of the hymns, Luke composed most of the material himself. According to Brown's reconstruction, the Lukan infancy narrative originally consisted of parallel stories about the announcements and births of John and Jesus, intentionally arranged in a diptych pattern. Although some scholars have suggested that independent Baptist sources or Mary traditions lie behind these stories, Brown does not find such suppositions necessary. The stories are modeled after accounts in the Old Testament. John's parents, for example, are constructed on the pattern of Abraham and Sarah, an elderly couple in want of a child.

The hymns that are found in Luke's infancy narrative include what are known today as the Magnificat (1:46–55), the Benedictus (1:68–79), and the Nunc Dimittis (2:29–32). Because of their strong Jewish orientation, scholars have often surmised that these are in fact Jewish psalms that Luke has taken over and adapted for Christian purposes. Brown, however, thinks it is more likely that they arose within an early Jewish-Christian setting. Luke must have found them and incorporated them into his infancy narrative at a somewhat late stage of composition, since they unbalance his otherwise neat pattern of diptychs concerning John and Jesus. Without disputing this, Stephen Farris suggests that the incorporation of these hymns gave the section a new pattern: each hymn now forms the third movement of a three-fold "promise-fulfillment-praise" cycle. In addition, Farris says that the hymns themselves express the themes of promise and fulfillment and the restoration of Israel, motifs that recur throughout Luke's composition. He supposes, then, that Luke placed these hymns at the front of his work so that, like an overture, they could sound themes that would be prominent throughout.[37]

2) *Stories and Parables.* Many of the New Testament's best-known parables are found only in Luke's Gospel. These include the Good Samaritan (10:25–37), the Friend at Midnight (11:5–10), the Rich Fool (12:13–21), the Prodigal Son (15:11–32), the Unjust Steward (16:1–13), the Rich Man and Lazarus (16:19–31), the Unrighteous Judge (18:1–8), and the Pharisee and the Tax-Collector (18:9–14). In addition, Luke contains a number of brief stories, such as the accounts of Mary and Martha (10:38–42) and Zacchaeus (19:1–10) that are found nowhere else.

Luke has placed almost all of these special stories and parables in the central section of his Gospel, the travel narrative. But where did he find such classic tales in the first place? According to John Drury, he may have composed them himself.[38] In his book, *The Parables in the Gospels*, Drury notes that the parables and parable-like stories that are unique to Luke have features in common. The crisis, for example, typically occurs in the middle of the tale rather than at the end as it does in parables found in the other Gospels. Also, Luke's parables are more concerned with the world of human beings: they pay more attention to characterization and are richer in human interest and homely detail. Luke's stories exhibit a greater realism and are marked by a diminution of the allegorical aspect that is so dominant elsewhere. Other distinctly Lukan features can be seen in the prominence of banquets and journeys and the attention paid to the rich and poor. It is in this material, then, that Luke may be exercising his greatest creativity as a writer.

This does not mean he composes without any sources at all. In fact, Drury believes that while scholars have been searching for Luke's "special source," it may very well have been staring them in the face all along. It is the Old Testament. Following the Jewish literary technique of midrash, Luke is able to imaginatively construct stories from the briefest of Old Testament allusions. For example, the story of the Good Samaritan could be a midrash on 2 Chronicles 28:14–15. In this passage it is said that, after armed men attacked a group of people from Judah, some men from Samaria came and "clothed them . . . provided them with food and drink and anointed them, and, carrying all the feeble among them on asses, they brought them to . . . Jericho." According to Drury, this brief historical note provided Luke with the essential elements for his much more developed illustrative tale. In other cases, Drury sees Luke's stories as mosaics of miscellaneous, previously unconnected Old Testament references.

In his book, *The Gospel in Parable*, John Donahue also sees the unique parables of Luke as being in harmony with the theological directions of the Gospel as a whole.[39] The realism of the stories and their concern with everyday life are reflective of Luke's shift in eschatology. Throughout his Gospel, Luke wants to shift the locus of salvation from the end-time to the everyday experience of Christian life. This is seen in Jesus' correction of those who suppose "the kingdom of God is to appear immediately" (19:11) and in the frequent occurrence throughout Luke of the word "today" or "daily" (4:21; 5:26; 9:23; 11:3; 13:32; 19:5, 9; 23:43). In his unique parables, then, the concern is not with the coming of the kingdom but with the earthly lives of everyday people. Donahue also finds in Luke's parables a summons to conversion and a theology of witness that is typical of the Gospel as a whole.

3) *The Passion Narrative.* It is obvious from a brief comparison of accounts that Luke's story of Jesus' passion differs remarkably from that found in either Mark or Mat-

thew. For example, in both of the latter Gospels, Jesus is reported as speaking only once from the cross, when he utters the cry of dereliction, "My God, my God, why have you forsaken me?" Luke not only omits this saying, but also introduces three more "words from the cross," which are not found anywhere else in the New Testament: "Father, forgive them, for they know not what they do" (23:34), "Truly, I say to you, today you will be with me in Paradise" (23:43), and "Father, into your hands I commit my spirit" (23:46).

Scholars have often wondered whether Luke possessed a story of Jesus' passion other than that contained in the Gospel of Mark. Numerous studies to determine the extent and origin of such a source have focused on the linguistic and stylistic aspects of the material, but, in general, the results of such studies have cancelled each other out without providing a clear solution.[40] Recently, studies have shifted their emphasis to thought-content and have examined the material in terms of Luke's overall redactional and compositional technique. Marion Soards applies this approach to chapter 22 of Luke's Gospel in his book, *The Passion According to Luke.*[41] The special material in this section, Soards finds, is not substantial enough to sustain a continuous narrative; rather, it seems to represent smaller independent units. Accordingly, he decides that Luke did not have any single, coherent source other than Mark. He redacted the Markan account by reordering the material, by adding bits of new information culled from oral tradition, and by freely composing some portions himself. All of this was done in accord with his distinctive theological purposes. In particular, he wants to show that the passion is the realization of a divine plan that inaugurates the last days. Jesus is shown to be in charge of the passion events and the disciples are portrayed as those in whom his prophecies are fulfilled. Through all of this, Luke's reader is instructed concerning the plan of God.

Frank Matera's study in *Passion Narratives and Gospel Theologies* is less meticulous but covers both chapters 22 and 23.[42] Matera also believes the unique elements of Luke's passion story express themes that are developed throughout his work. For example, Luke's portrayal of Jesus as being in control of the events reinforces the notion that the passion is his destiny. This idea is also expressed in the long travel narrative (9:51–19:44), which has Jerusalem as its goal, and in the repeated affirmation that "it is necessary" for Jesus to suffer (9:22, 44; 17:25; 24:7, 26, 44). Luke also presents his version of the passion as a final lesson in discipleship, one that culminates the teaching Jesus has been giving his disciples all along. In going to his death, Jesus shows them what it means to be a servant, to face trials, and to take up one's cross. Finally, Luke tells the passion story in such a way that Jesus is seen to be God's rejected Prophet as well as God's royal Son. Matera believes that these two portraits, Jesus as Prophet and Jesus as the royal Son of God, are representative of the christology expressed throughout Luke's narrative.

In short, it appears that the special themes of Luke's passion story may be considered reflective of the evangelist's own theological interests. This is true even of the three "words from the cross" mentioned above. Jesus' prayer for his executioners (23:34), while textually uncertain, presents his death as a model of discipleship: he has previously taught his disciples to pray for those who abuse them (6:28). His word to the thief (23:43) emphasizes the "daily" presence of salvation that is stressed elsewhere (2:11; 4:21; 5:26; 19:9), just as the reference to his kingdom (23:42) points to his royal identity. Finally, when Jesus prays, "Father, into your hands I commit my spirit" (23:46), he simultaneously affirms his divine sonship and his noble acceptance of the passion as his destiny.

## Luke and Acts

Since it is usually recognized that Luke is the author of the book of Acts as well as our third Gospel, students of his compositional technique are interested in comparing the two works. Charles Talbert does this in his book, *Literary Patterns, Theological Themes, and the Genre of Luke-Acts*, and he finds they are even more closely related than they may at first appear.[43]

Talbert calls attention to parallels between the Gospel and Acts that indicate they have been composed according to the same general pattern. Obviously, both works begin with a stereotypical preface (Lk 1:1–4; Acts 1:1–5). Early in the Gospel, the Spirit descends upon Jesus at his baptism (3:22) and, in Acts, the apostles are also baptized with the Holy Spirit (2:24). In the respective books, both Jesus and the apostles embark on ministries of preaching and healing and both are brought into conflict with the religious leaders. Parallels can also be seen between Jesus' journey to Jerusalem (9:51–19:28) and the missionary journeys of Paul, especially the final one, which ends in Jerusalem (Acts 19:21–21:17). The story of Jesus' trial, in which he is shuttled back and forth between various rulers, also corresponds to the trial of Paul with which the book of Acts concludes.

These general correspondences between the Gospel and Acts are interesting enough, but Talbert digs deeper and finds that at times the two works even correspond in specific detail. For example, Jesus' healing of a lame man in Luke 5:17–26 matches the healing of a lame man in his name in Acts 3:1-10. Similarly, both Jesus and Peter are invited to the house of a Roman centurion (Lk 7:1-10; Acts 10). In their respective trials, both Jesus (Lk 23:4, 14, 22) and Paul (Acts 23:9; 25:25; 26:31) are declared to be innocent three times. The presence of such detailed correspondences convinces Talbert that Luke must have begun his two-volume work with some sort of preliminary plan. The organization or "architecture" of the work shows careful, even meticulous plotting, such as is evident in other literary masterpieces of the period. In fact, further investigation shows that Luke has applied a similar scheme on a smaller scale in the organization of sections and sub-sections within the two books. There are, for example, remarkable parallels between Luke 9 and Luke 22-23 and between Acts 1-12 and Acts 13-28. Talbert suggests that the function of such an elaborate compositional technique was partly aesthetic, but would also serve as an assist to memory for the readers and hearers of the day. In addition, the patterns help to interpret the works' meaning. At the very least, the literary correspondences between Luke and Acts indicate a conviction that is unique to this evangelist, namely, that both the story of Jesus and the story of the Church are incomplete without the other.

**Observations and Conclusions**

This chapter has attempted to map current discussion concerning the sources and compositional techniques that have informed Luke's Gospel. It may be helpful to reconsider some of what has been said in terms of the models proposed in the last chapter. Scholars sometimes approach Luke differently, regarding the evangelist as a historian, as a theologian, or as a literary artist.

Scholars like John Kloppenborg and Richard Edwards are interested in Luke as a historian, for they consider his Gospel to be a valuable resource for recovering the otherwise lost Q source. In the studies discussed here, at least, they are interested in what Luke did with Q primarily so that they can un-do it and get back to a more original layer of tradition. Another important scholar, James Robinson has called Q "the most important Christian document we have" and has formed a group dedicated to its eventual reconstruction.[44] William Farmer has problems with both the methodological presuppositions and canonical implications of such an enterprise, for he dreads the day when some may seek to place in the pews reconstructed copies of a document, which, in his view, never existed.[45]

Most scholars are interested in Luke's use of sources because of the light this throws on understanding the evangelist as a theologian. A fairly standard methodology has developed by which scholars like Joseph Fitzmyer, Jan Lambrecht, and Helmuth Egelkraut examine Luke's redaction of material drawn from Mark or Q in an effort to discern his particular theological tendencies. Lately, however, a lack of scholarly consensus concerning the validity of the Two-Source Hypothesis has limited the acceptance of this approach. Although the majority of scholars continue to work with the established model (as the remainder of this book will show), they do so with the frustrating awareness that their results will be regarded by some as tenuous.

It is this frustration, perhaps, that has contributed to a growing interest in approaches that view Luke as a literary artist. Charles Talbert's study on Luke-Acts and some of the studies on Luke's special material discussed in this chapter represent this tendency toward focusing on literary patterns and theological motifs that can be discerned within the work as a whole. These studies often do not presuppose any particular source theory, but pay more attention to broad literary techniques and compositional factors. Although the interest is still, ultimately, in Luke as a theologian, the trend in these studies is to view him more as an author than as an editor.

# 3
# The Concerns of Luke's Community

The location of Luke's community cannot be determined, for even in ancient times the traditions varied greatly.[1] Nevertheless, scholars believe they can discern some of the issues that faced Luke's Church from clues within his writings. The book of Acts is considered a great asset here, for, if anything, community concerns are more transparent there than in the Gospel. The belief is that whatever can be learned about Luke's community from either of his volumes will be helpful in interpreting them both.

## The Problem of the Parousia

It has already been indicated that Hans Conzelmann, in his classic synthesis of Luke's theology,[2] identifies the pivotal problem facing the evangelist as the historical delay of the parousia. The chief evidence for this contention is the existence of the book of Acts itself, for, as others have said, "you do not write the history of the Church if you are expecting the end of the world to come any day."[3] There are also apparent references to a period of delay scattered throughout Luke's writings (e.g., 12:38, 45; 19:11; 21:24). According to Conzelmann's reconstruction, Jesus and the early Christians expected the parousia to occur very soon, certainly within their own generation. When this did not happen, the Church was faced with a theological crisis of monumental proportions.

Conzelmann believes it is this problem that motivates Luke to develop his scheme of salvation history. Luke seeks to eradicate the expectation of an imminent end by positing a prolonged and divinely-ordained "Age of the Church." The consequences of such a theological shift are numerous: the basis for ethics must be reinterpreted, the relationship of Church and society must be investigated, mission goals must be established, and the rightful place of Spirit and tradition in the life of the Church must be considered. In short, Conzelmann believes that the starting point for understanding Luke's theology is his concept of salvation history, and that this concept, in turn, is occasioned by the problem of the parousia.

Impressive as it is, Conzelmann's proposal has not fared well in recent years. There are even a few (though not many) scholars who think he has gotten it precisely backwards. A. J. Mattill argues in his book *Luke and the Last Things* that the evangelist writes with fervency because he believes the parousia is imminent.[4] In Luke's Gospel, Jesus instructs his followers to proclaim the nearness of the Kingdom of God (10:9, 11) and promises to return as a sign to "this generation" (11:30; 21:32). In the book of Acts, the final judgment is referred to as something that will happen "before long" or "soon" (Acts 17:31; 24:15, 25).[5] Mattill finds Luke's works to be replete with apocalyptic imagery and so concludes that the evangelist believes the final holy war has already begun. He writes to give the Church new impetus for its task now that the end is in sight.

Many other writers have noted the texts Mattill cites and attempted to reconcile them with the delay theme expounded by Conzelmann. Is it not possible for Luke to regard the parousia as delayed without abandoning the thought that it is still imminent? Hans Bartsch has tried to work out such a two-sided approach in his book, *Wachet aber zu jeder Zeit*.[6] The title takes its cue from Luke 21:36 ("Watch at all times") and points to what Bartsch considers to be Luke's main concern with regard to the parousia. It does belong to the indefinite future, but this does not mean it is postponed. Precisely because the future is indefinite, the parousia is always imminent. Luke does not necessarily foresee a prolonged era of the Church; what he does envision is a Church that lives forever on the edge. Accordingly, if the delay of the parousia has caused a problem for Luke, it is not disappointment but laxity. Luke wants to renew the eschatological awareness, not dispel it. At the same time, however, he is careful to identify the parousia as an event that is still to come. According to 2 Tim 2:18, there were some in the early Church who believed the final resurrection was already past. Luke, therefore, must postpone the parousia for some and proclaim its imminence for others. The apparent ambiguity is resolved when it is seen that he is fighting on two fronts.[7]

The criticism leveled against Conzelmann by all those discussed so far is that he fails to deal with a significant strand of the Lukan material, namely those passages that do represent the end as near. Another, more broadly-based critique would be that he fails to consider alternative motives for Luke's enterprise. Even those who agree with his perception that Luke postpones the parousia tend to fault him on this account: he exaggerates the significance of the problem. Some scholars believe that Luke inherited the idea of an extended interval from his sources.[8] Others ask whether he did not simply acknowledge it as a fact of history without any attendant theological trauma.[9] The development of the salvation-history scheme can be accounted for on other grounds.[10]

In short, and on this scholars seem to agree, it was not the delay itself that constituted a major concern for Luke, but, rather, what happened during the delay. False teachers arose and led people astray. The community suffered from persecution and tribulation. The Jerusalem headquarters was destroyed and the mission to Israel all but came to a halt. Meanwhile, Gentiles accepted the Gospel in surprising numbers, changing the whole social fabric of the movement. Whatever Luke's views about the future might have been, there were plenty of matters in the present that demanded his immediate attention.

### False Teaching

Charles H. Talbert argues in his book *Luke and the Gnostics* that the major purpose of Luke-Acts is to provide a defense against false teaching in the Church.[11] Specifically, the heresies that Luke combats are those ideas usually associated with Gnosticism.[12] As Talbert sees it, the Gnostic system was based on an extreme dualism that projected a Docetic view of Christ. Holding that all matter and flesh is inherently evil, the Gnostic teachers described Christ as a spiritual being who did not actually suffer or die. The idea of bodily resurrection was especially abhorrent to them because they considered salvation to be an escape from the wretchedness of the body. These teachers appealed to their own peculiar exegesis of the Old Testament and had some influence in the first century, as can be seen by attacks against them in other New Testament writings.[13]

Talbert notes that Luke's Gospel presents Jesus in such a way as to discount these ideas. Luke identifies the Christ with the human Jesus (4:16–24; 6:1–5; 7:27–30; 20:17–18), emphasizes the necessity that he suffer, die, and rise again (9:22, 44–45; 17:25; 18:31–34; 22:37; 24:6–11; 24:25–27), and affirms the general resurrection to come (20:37).[14] But Luke does not stop there. He goes to great lengths to establish the apostles as authentic witnesses to Jesus' life, death, and resurrection and to present them as the legitimate interpreters of Scripture. Thus he intends to pull the rug out from under those who come up with interpretations and revelations of their own. For Luke's Church, there is a legitimate succession of tradition based on the testimony of reliable witnesses. The level of concern that Luke shows for the authenticity of tradition presupposes that there were some traditions that he considered inauthentic.

Once it is recognized that Luke is combating Gnostics, there are several passages in his writings that take on new meaning. Talbert suggests, for instance, that the story of the virgin birth may not testify so much to Jesus' spiritual origins as to the fact that he has a human parent. Similarly, the genealogy makes it clear that being the Son of God does not separate Jesus from his human lineage (cf. 3:38). Again, the resurrection appearances in Luke stress the physicality of the risen Lord: Jesus eats with his disciples and emphasizes that, unlike a spirit, he has "flesh and bones" (24:39–43).

## Tribulation

When Luke records Paul as saying, "Through many tribulations we must enter the Kingdom of God" (Acts 14:22), it is likely that he has the situation of his own community in mind. In Luke's Gospel, Jesus predicts that Christians will have to endure terrible afflictions on his account, including social ostracism (6:22; 21:16–17) and violent persecution (11:49; 21:12). The book of Acts offers abundant examples of such predictions being fulfilled.

In one way or another, most of the New Testament

writings deal with the theme of "faith under fire." According to Schuyler Brown, however, Luke treats this theme in a distinctive way.[15] In his book *Apostasy and Perseverance in the Theology of Luke*, Brown notes that it is not the faith of the individual Christian that is under fire for Luke so much as the faith of the Church. Luke is concerned to demonstrate that the Church has persevered in time of tribulation and not given way to apostasy. Although Jesus' disciples do not understand why it is necessary for him to die, in Luke's Gospel they do not abandon him and run away as they do in Matthew and Mark. Similarly, Peter's denial that he knows Jesus (22:34) does not constitute a denial of Jesus himself (cf. Mt 26:34; Mk 14:30). He falls victim to the sin of cowardice, but his faith does not fail (22:32). The only true example of apostasy among the founders of the Church is that of Judas, and this is swiftly repaired through the election of Matthias (Acts 1:15–26). Luke presents the apostles as standing by Jesus in trials (22:28) so that they may provide a faithful link between the time of Jesus and the time of the Church.

Another distinctive feature of Luke's approach to tribulation is that he entertains no notion of suffering as the means through which God tests and purifies the faith of Christians (cf. 2 Cor 1:8–9; 1 Pet 1:6–7). On the contrary, it is Satan who puts people to the test and this is something that every faithful Christian should avoid (11:4; 22:40, 46). Luke does not consider suffering from the perspective of the individual Christian and he does not regard it as a potentially redemptive challenge. Rather, he considers the tribulations of the Church to be a diabolical onslaught conducted by evil people who, under Satan's influence, intend to thwart God's plan of salvation. The devil's scheme fails, however, when the Church perseveres in tribulation and, if anything, continues its mission with renewed vigor.

Though Luke's primary concern is to assure the reliability of the witnesses on which his Gospel depends, he establishes norms for facing tribulation in his own day as well. As with the apostles, perseverance is to be understood in terms of an unfailing conviction rather than a particular strength of character. Just as the apostles stood by Jesus in his trials, the Christians of Luke's day are called to stand by the word of the Lord that the apostles bequeathed to them. Thus Luke conceives of faithfulness in collective rather than individualistic terms. The victory of the suffering Christian is not determined by the outcome of an inner struggle but by the outcome of the cosmic struggle between the world and the Church, that is, between the sphere of Satan and the sphere of God's Holy Spirit. The Christian perseveres not by proving his or her faith but by remaining in the strong faith of the Church.

If Brown thinks Luke refers suffering Christians to the Church, David Tiede believes he directs them to the Scriptures. In his book *Prophecy and History in Luke-Acts*, Tiede demonstrates how Luke turned to the Old Testament to make sense of the tribulations of his day.[16] The answers Luke finds are paradoxical: suffering comes as a result of faithfulness and of sin.

The sufferings of Jesus and the early Christians testify to their faithfulness to God. Like the "suffering servant" of Isaiah and the rejected prophets of Israel, Jesus and his followers accept their persecution as a necessary part of God's plan. It is intrinsically true that no prophet will ever be accepted by those to whom the prophet is sent, for the true prophet's message is a challenge to basic self-understanding. Knowing this, Jesus is able to speak of his rejection in a proleptic sense, responding to people as though they have rejected him even before they actually do so (4:22–24).

The main focus of Tiede's book, however, is on the

tribulation that Luke's community experiences in a broader context. Tiede believes that Luke writes for a predominantly Jewish-Christian community, one that shares in the sufferings of the whole Jewish nation. Shortly before Luke's Gospel was written, the Jews were involved in a disastrous war with Rome: the "people of God" were humiliated and their Temple was destroyed. Like other Jewish groups, the Jewish Christians asked, "How could such a thing happen?" It was not, however, the first time such a thing had happened. The Temple had been destroyed before and, in their Scriptures, the Jewish people found prophetic interpretations of that event which spoke with new relevance now. From these Scriptures Luke concludes that, unlike the tribulations of Jesus and the early Christians, the plight of Israel was not due to faithfulness; it was due to sin. Israel's past suffering could be correlated with its failure to heed the prophets God had sent. Similarly, the present suffering could be attributed to Israel's rejection of the Messiah.

What all of this means for Luke and his community is that their present distress is a part of God's plan. In keeping with divine intention, Jesus came as both herald and agent of God's reign. As was necessary, he and his followers were rejected by Israel, which brought about the current "days of vengeance." This is not the end, however, for according to Scripture, divine punishment is preliminary to the vindication of God's people. For the present, it seems that God has turned to the Gentiles, but this is just a prophetic reproof of Israel. After the "time of the Gentiles" has been fulfilled, God's promises to Israel will also be accomplished and Israel will be restored.

In short, Tiede believes that Luke finds a divine pattern of prophecy/rejection/punishment/vindication in the Hebrew Scriptures and that he interprets the tribulation of his community and nation in this light. The Jewish Christians have experienced rejection and, ironically, must now share the suffering that has come upon all Jewish people as a result of that rejection. By showing his community that all this happens in fulfillment of Scripture, Luke offers assurance that God's plan is in fact working as it should and that, accordingly, the ultimate promise of vindication will not fail.

A comparison of Brown and Tiede reveals that both scholars believe Luke wrote his Gospel for a community that had experienced suffering and tribulation. Brown, however, identifies this tribulation with the persecution of the Christian Church while Tiede puts more emphasis on the effects of the Jewish war. For Brown, Luke is concerned with the question of how the Church responds to tribulation; for Tiede, the question is why such tribulation comes in the first place. As Brown sees it, Luke's community looks to the past for assurance in times of difficulty and trusts in the reliable witness of a Church that has persevered. Tiede represents Luke and his community as looking to the future, where the promises of God will be fulfilled. But the most striking difference between these two presentations is that Brown interprets Luke as writing for a community of overcomers, while Tiede envisions a community that experiences rejection and defeat. In Brown's view, the Church has persevered through many trials and is currently engaged in a triumphal mission that can not be hindered by Satan's attacks. Tiede reconstructs a community for Luke that comprises the lowest of the low. These Jewish Christians are not winners, but two-time losers: they suffer not only from the humiliation of the Jewish people by Rome, but from rejection by other Jews as well.

How can two portraits of Luke's community present such different versions of its approach to adversity? The explanation is connected, in part, to the question of whether Luke writes primarily for Jews or Gentiles. Since Brown assumes the latter, he does not consider that the setbacks of Jews (or even of Jewish Christians) would be of much moment for Luke and his Church. Tiede, on the other hand, envisions a Lukan community of Jewish Christians, for whom the successes of the Gentile mission cannot ameliorate the harsh reality of their own situation.

## Jews and Gentiles

Whatever the ethnic composition of Luke's community, it is certain that they faced the question of how Gentile Christianity relates to Judaism.[17] Many scholars believe that Luke himself was a Gentile and that in his day Christianity had become, by and large, a Gentile religion. Nevertheless, the founders of this religion and most of its heroes of faith had been Jews. How could the present situation and the traditional heritage be reconciled?

In his book *The Purpose of Luke-Acts*, Robert Maddox notes that there is a sustained development of the theme, "Israel and the Gentiles" from Luke 1 through Acts 28.[18] It is obviously a pressing concern for the evangelist and his community. Maddox believes this is because the Jewish community of Luke's day was challenging the legitimacy of Gentile Christianity. The question, quite simply, was "Who are the true people of God?" Luke does not take up this question in order to convince the Jewish critics themselves, but, rather, to resolve the identity crisis that their propaganda has caused within his community. He wants to explain to Christians their historical situation and the nature of their existence as an institution apart from Judaism.

How does Luke do this? He shows that by rejecting Jesus and the early Christian missionaries, Judaism has also rejected God's plan of salvation. Accordingly, the Jewish people have been judged by God and, for the most part, excluded from the fulfillment of God's ancestral promises. Those promises will now be fulfilled for the people who accept them, namely the Gentile Christians. In Luke's view, such a development is not strange, for the entire history of Israel can be read as one long tale of rebellion against God: even the building of the Temple was an act of defiance (Acts 7:41–53).

Maddox's understanding of this theme explains different elements of Luke's Gospel. He detects, for example, a "Jewish orientation" in Luke that accentuates the Jewishness of Jesus and other exemplary figures. At the same time, however, there is an "anti-Jewish orientation" that presents Jesus' oracles of judgment against Jerusalem and highlights the role of the Jewish leaders in Jesus' execution. Luke's purpose is to demonstrate the essential continuity between Christianity and the Jewish hope, while at the same time offering an explanation as to why that hope is not fulfilled for Israel. Luke answers the charges of his critics by proclaiming that it is the Jews rather than the Christians who are the heretics and apostates.

Many of these same themes are also noted by Stephen G. Wilson in his study, *The Gentiles and the Gentile Mission in Luke-Acts.*[19] Whereas Maddox emphasizes the rejection of the Christian message by the Jewish people, however, Wilson stresses the acceptance of salvation by Gentiles. Luke is concerned to show that the Gentile mission was not just "a bright idea of the early church," and that it did not develop as a mere quirk of history. Rather, the origin of the mission is to be found in the words and actions of Jesus. In Luke 24:46–49, the risen Jesus tells his disciples that repentance and forgiveness of sins is to be preached in his name "to all nations." Furthermore, he ties this command to Old Testament prophecy so that the mission to the Gentiles is grounded in the eternal will of God. It is viewed as an integral part of God's plan from the beginning. A careful reading of the Gospel reveals that this theme is developed consistently throughout: Simeon prophesies that Jesus will be "a light to the Gentiles" (2:32) and the coming of John the Baptist means that "all flesh will see the salvation of God" (3:6). Luke does not anachronistically present Jesus as pursuing a Gentile mission during his own lifetime, but he does make it clear that such a mission is part of God's plan.

Wilson explores another aspect of this issue in his second monograph, *Luke and the Law*.[20] The influx of Gentiles into the Christian Church raised critical questions about the validity of the Jewish law. From his study of Luke's Gospel, however, Wilson concludes that this was pretty much a settled issue for the evangelist's community.[21] The variety and ambiguity of the material on the law in Luke is more evidence of his indifference toward the problem than anything else. For example, Jesus is sometimes presented as staunchly upholding the law (11:42; 16:17) but at other times he seems to supplement (16:18; 18:22) or challenge (6:1–5; 9:59–60) it. This does not bother Luke because he is not particularly concerned with Jesus' attitude or practice regarding the law; these passages are significant to him for other reasons and what they say about the law is incidental.

Luke's concept, which no doubt reflects the view of his community, is that the Jewish law is the custom of a particular people (in Greek, the *ethos* of an *ethnos*). The theological basis for this lies in the concept that God is not partisan, that is, that God makes no distinction between Jews and Gentiles. But Luke's interest here is more pragmatic than theological: the customs of the Jews are not the customs of the Gentiles. Living according to the law was natural for the earlier Jewish Christians, but it would not be natural or appropriate for the Gentile Christians of his own time. There are, of course, certain fundamental beliefs and moral commitments from Judaism that are basic to all Christians because they were affirmed by Jesus and the apostles. Love of God and neighbor (10:27) is one. The "apostolic decree" in Acts 15:22–29 can also be interpreted in this context. For the most part, however, Luke's community assumes that Gentiles have their own type of piety and that it is just as good as that of the Jews. In the final analysis, being a Jew or a Gentile brings no advantage, for both must rely for salvation exclusively on Christ (Acts 15:11).

Jack T. Sanders, another scholar who has tackled this question, is not convinced that Luke is so open-minded. In his book, *The Jews in Luke-Acts*, he makes explicit what is perhaps implied in Maddox's analysis: Luke is anti-semitic.[22] Sanders agrees with Maddox that Luke highlights the Jewish rejection of Christianity, but he believes the motivation for doing so is more polemical than apologetic. Luke has moved beyond assuring Gentile Christians of the legitimacy of their faith to attacking the validity of other persuasions. His hostility, furthermore, is not reserved simply for those Jews who reject the Christian message, but is directed also against those who accept it. It is Jewish Christians who are his target.

Sanders notes, first of all, the "blanket condemnations" in Luke's writings, according to which the Jews are by nature obstreperous and opposed to the will of God. It is significant that these condemnations typically occur in the speeches of the major characters, while the narrative material is more benign. Luke uses the discourse sections to interpret the narrative, which otherwise might be read as attributing the opposition to Israel's leaders and representing the people in general as more receptive to Jesus. For example, although in Luke's passion narrative it is primarily the Jewish leaders who are responsible for putting Jesus to death, Paul is able to say in Acts that this was done by "those who live in Jerusalem and their rulers" (Acts 13:27). Similarly, during his ministry, Jesus calls the Jews an "evil generation" (11:29) and he regards them as people who have rejected him even before they actually do so (4:23).

Luke is not simply giving vent to vague religious and ethnic bigotry. He is motivated by a specific threat to the Gentile Christian community of his day. Sanders finds the clue to such a threat in Acts 15:5, where Luke speaks of Christian Pharisees who insist that Gentile believers must be circumcised and keep the law of Moses. Accordingly, Sanders would disagree with Wilson that the law is a settled issue for Luke's community. He believes that Luke is compelled to defend his community against "Judaizers," similar, perhaps, to those whom Paul confronts in his letter to the Galatians. Luke makes his case by writing a story in which the Jewish Pharisees of Jesus' day stand for the Christian Pharisees of his own. The Pharisees in Luke's Gospel are hypocrites (12:1) who appear to be true believers but in reality promote self-justification and self-exaltation (16:15; 18:9–14). In Luke's view, there is a direct parallel between these opponents of Jesus, who repeatedly challenge him regarding matters of law, and the Jewish Christians who afflict his own community concerning similar issues.

In short, Luke does not differentiate greatly between Jewish Christians and other Jews; the Judaizers of his day are cut from the same cloth as the Jews who killed Jesus. Is it even possible, in his mind, for Jews to become Christians? Perhaps, Sanders admits, but only if they are willing to deny the validity of their own traditions and accept Christianity as a Gentile religion. In general, though, Luke believes "the world will be better off when the Jews get what they deserve and the world is rid of them."[23]

It can be seen that, although scholars disagree on the particulars, there is consensus that the presence of Gentiles in Luke's community has had a significant effect on his theology. Maddox thinks the situation necessitated a defense against attacks from without. Wilson believes it brought about a re-evaluation of tradition, according to which those elements that seemed to justify the current situation were highlighted and those that seemed irrelevant to it were ignored. Sanders maintains that the presence of Gentiles in Luke's community precipitated a division that led to polemics even against other Christians.

Jacob Jervell is the best known representative of a completely different school of thought. In his book *Luke and the People of God*, Jervell challenges the assumption that Luke writes primarily for Gentile Christians.[24] He admits that the Gentile mission is an important concern for the evangelist, but believes that Luke evaluates it from the point of view of Jewish Christianity.

As such, Jervell disagrees with many of the ideas expressed above, especially the suggestion that, for Luke, it is the Jewish rejection of Christianity that prompts the Gentile mission. Luke does not represent the Jewish people as rejecting the Christian message, but in fact portrays the mission to the Jews as a fabulous success. The book of Acts reports mass conversions of Jews to Christianity (2:41; 4:4; 6:7) until finally it can be said that "myriads" of Jews who "are zealous for the law" are among the believers (21:20). The Gentile mission, furthermore, is conducted within the sphere of Jewish Christianity and its success is viewed as a sign that the Jewish Christians are right. According to Jervell, Luke links the Gentile mission to the Jews' acceptance of Christianity rather than to their rejection of it.

Indeed, Jervell believes that, for Luke, Christianity is and must remain a Jewish entity, for "outside Israel, there is no salvation." Even within Israel salvation is not assured, for the Scriptures have long prophesied that when Israel is restored, the unrepentant will be excluded. In Luke's view, the Jewish Christians (and there are many) represent the restored Israel, while those Jews who reject the Gospel are the excluded ones. The essential division, therefore, is not between Israel and the Gentiles but within Israel itself.

Still, in Luke's day there is a Gentile mission and large numbers of Gentiles are coming into the Church. How is this to be interpreted by a Jewish Christian community? Once again, the Scriptures have foretold that when Israel is restored, even the Gentiles will repent. From Luke's perspective, then, the restoration of Israel is already an accomplished fact and the influx of Gentiles attests to this. The Gentile mission does not represent a break with Israel, but an affirmation of Israel. Luke views his community as consisting of "a people and an associate people," that is of Jewish Christians who represent the chosen people of God and of Gentile Christians who are being granted a special share in their salvation. There is no thought that the promises to Israel have been transferred to the Church, or that the Gentiles form a substitute for the lost people of God. The promises given to Israel are being fulfilled for the obedient Jews who believe in Jesus. One of those promises is the salvation of the Gentiles.

Although Jervell has worked primarily with the book of Acts, his proposal contributes a significant framework for understanding Luke's Gospel as well. Certainly the passages concerning Jesus' disputes over the law, his cleansing of the Temple, and his execution by the Jewish leaders must be read differently if the Gospel is written for a predominantly Jewish-Christian community instead of for a Gentile one. It is noteworthy that, while Jervell's perspective is at variance with what he calls "the common view," an increasing body of scholarship, including the work of David Tiede discussed above, is indebted to his interpretation.[25]

## Observations and Conclusions

Although there is widespread discussion regarding the concerns of Luke's community, a few points of agreement may be noted. For one thing, all of the scholars discussed in this chapter assume Luke is writing for people within the Church. Other views are occasionally proposed: that the books are evangelistic;[26] that they were prepared to serve as a defense for Paul at his trial;[27] or, that they are an appeal to Rome to recognize Christianity as a legal religion.[28] None of these suggestions has found sustained support.

It can also be said that scholars identify the principal concerns of Luke-Acts as falling within the realms of eschatology and ecclesiology (increasingly, the latter). Luke's theology is not abstract, but eminently practical. He approaches great theological themes with a pragmatic prejudice. He develops theology in response to the needs and challenges of his own Church.

Finally, as noted above, the attention that scholars are giving to temporal concerns (false teaching, tribulation, and the relationship of Jews and Gentiles) reflects a consensus that Conzelmann's emphasis on the delay of the parousia was overdrawn. It must be noted, however, that if Luke did not expect the parousia to come soon, this perspective would certainly have exacerbated the need to deal with other concerns, for they could not be regarded as problems that would soon be resolved by divine intervention. The delay theme may still have a place, then, as one factor among many affecting Luke's outlook, though not all scholars are willing to grant that he perceives a delay.

The greatest point of divergence is found on the question of whether Luke writes primarily for Jews or Gentiles. In this regard, an increasing number of scholars are content to eliminate the term "primarily" altogether and simply affirm that Luke writes for a mixed ethnic community, both elements of which require his attention.

# 4
# Christ and Salvation
# in the Gospel of Luke

All scholars would agree that the heart of Luke's theology is his understanding of Jesus. It is sometimes debated whether his view of Christ has determined his approach to other religious matters or vice versa, but no one would doubt that the two are inseparable. One scholar sums up the evangelist's perspective in a phrase: "Christology is ecclesiology, and ecclesiology is christology."[1] All of the community concerns discussed in the last chapter are addressed, not through epistles after the fashion of Paul, but through a story that tells about Jesus and his influence on people.

The most basic issue for Lukan studies is this: What does Luke think about Jesus? Scholars have approached this question in a variety of ways and, not surprisingly, have come up with some different answers.

## Christological Titles

One approach to Luke's christology has been to analyze the titles and names ascribed to Jesus in his writings. These include the following: Christ (Messiah), King (of the Jews), Lord, Master, Prophet, Savior, Servant, Son of

David, Son of God, Son of Man, and Teacher. A wealth of periodical literature has been devoted to the meaning of these terms.[2]

On the basis of this research, a few interesting observations can be made. Statistically, Luke's favorite titles are "Christ" and "Lord." He sometimes likes to combine these two (2:11; Acts 2:36) and, in one instance, links them both to another, "Savior" (2:11). This latter term is significant because, aside from a single reference in John (4:42), Luke is the only evangelist who uses it for Jesus. Luke drops the title "Son of God" from the centurion's affirmation of Jesus at the cross (23:47; cf. Mark 15:39), but introduces it, with a different sense, into his story of the virgin birth (1:32, 35). It is also interesting to note which titles are used by whom: in Luke, only Jesus' disciples call him "Master," though people in general may identify him as "a prophet" (7:16; 9:19). On the other hand, the disciples never call Jesus "Teacher," a term reserved for inquirers and opponents. As in the other Gospels, the title "Son of Man" is used only by Jesus himself, though in the book of Acts Luke records the only exception to this in the New Testament (7:36).

Jack Dean Kingsbury has attempted to interpret some of this data in his book *Jesus Christ in Matthew, Mark, and Luke*.[3] Although Luke uses a great many names for Jesus, Kingsbury believes the central confessional title for the Gospel is "the Christ (Messiah) of God." This can be seen in the climactic declaration of Peter (9:26), whose confession provides the best answer to a series of questions concerning Jesus' identity (5:21; 7:49; 8:25; 9:7–9; 9:18, 20). As the Christ of God, Jesus may also be called "King (of the Jews)" and "Son of David," but these titles are subject to possible misinterpretation. Luke must guard against the notion that Jesus is a political pretender who seeks to establish a Jewish state or that he wields Davidic authority in order to foment revolution. Rather, as the promised Messiah from the royal line of David, he is the bearer of God's eschatological rule (11:20; 19:38), through whom entrance into the sphere of God's reign is available (23:42–43).

Although "Christ of God" is Luke's most important title for Jesus, it must be supplemented in important ways. First, Peter's confession that Jesus is the Christ of God must be understood in terms of the rest of the story, which shows that this means Jesus is the one whom God has chosen to suffer and to rise so that salvation might be preached in his name (1:32–23, 35; 24:25–27, 46–47). Furthermore, Peter's confession is supplemented by God's own declaration, "This is my Son, my Chosen" (9:35, cf. 3:22). As the story of the virgin birth illustrates, Luke utilizes the title "Son of God" to focus on the unique relationship that exists between God the Father and Jesus the royal Messiah (1:32, 35). This unique relationship is also brought out by the titles "Lord" and "Savior," both of which can be used interchangeably for God and Jesus. The story of the temptation (4:1–13) reveals another aspect of Jesus' divine sonship: the essential ingredient of oneness with God is absolute obedience to the Father's will. Accordingly, Luke identifies Jesus as both the Son of God and the Servant of God and he calls attention to this by using the Greek term *pais*, which can mean either "son" or "servant."

In short, Kingsbury believes Luke sees Jesus as the Christ of God, but also as something more. This "more" may be understood in terms of the unique relationship with God ascribed to Jesus through the expressions Son of God and Servant of God. It is through Jesus, the royal Messiah, the Son and Servant of God, that God proffers salvation to Israel and, ultimately, to the Gentiles as well.

Finally, Kingsbury considers the title "Son of Man," which must be distinguished from the others as a non-confessional title. In Luke, as in Matthew and Mark, it is the name Jesus uses for himself as he interacts in public. He is never confessed or even addressed as the Son of Man by others. This title, then, does not express who Jesus is or reveal his identity to those who hear him use the term. At Jesus' ascension, however, Luke believes that Jesus enters into his glory and the "Son of Man" is identified as the Messiah Son of God (22:66–71; cf. Acts 7:56). Luke differs from Matthew and Mark in this regard, for they both represent this final identification as taking place at the parousia (Mark 14:61–62; Matt 26:63–64).

## Models from the Greco-Roman World

Another means of approaching Luke's christology has been to interpret his presentation of Jesus against the background of the Greco-Roman world. How would Luke's contemporaries have understood his Gospel? Is there any comparable literature of the day that suggests how this story of Jesus might have been received?

Charles Talbert, who has done extensive study on the genre of the Gospels, believes there are similarities between Luke's work and Hellenistic biographies of philosophers.[4] He calls attention to an early third-century work by Diogenes Laetrius called *Lives of Eminent Philosophers*. The subjects whom Laetrius selects for review are all regarded as divine figures: the philosophers are pictured as wandering preachers whose journeys are sometimes the result of divine command. Furthermore, Laetrius' biographies focus not only on the founders of philosophical schools but also on the masters' successors, who form a type of religious community that venerates the divine founder and is sustained by him. There is a particular concern with proper succession, in order to designate where it is that the "living voice" of the philosopher is still heard today. The philosophy itself, furthermore, is always explained as a way of living rather than as abstract speculation, and it is to be learned through imitation of the philosopher's own lifestyle as much as by remembering his precepts. If biographies like these were popular in Luke's time, Talbert concludes, readers of his Gospel would certainly relate Jesus to the Greco-Roman image of the wandering philosopher.

This model, however, does not exhaust the possibilities for understanding Luke's Jesus. Talbert suggests another image as well, namely the mythology of "immortals" in the Mediterranean world.[5] Immortals (like Dionysus or Hercules) were considered to be divine beings, but they were distinguished from the gods (like Zeus) who were eternal. Most immortals had been begotten through the union of a god or goddess with a human being and, originally mortal, they underwent a transformation at some point in their career to become immortal. Usually this transformation involved a visible ascent into heaven and was confirmed by subsequent appearances to the hero's friends or disciples. After he had been deified, the immortal could and did intervene on behalf of others. Given this background, Talbert thinks there is no way a Mediterranean person could read Luke's Gospel without seeing in Jesus the portrayal of an immortal.

There are differences, of course, between Luke's writings, which respect Jewish monotheism, and the pagan works of Greece and Rome. Still, Talbert believes that the combined image of the wandering philosopher and the immortal furnishes the best model for understanding the Lukan Jesus.[6] He is a divine teacher who calls disciples to emulate a new way of life and who, after ascending to glory, continues to intervene for the community that succeeds him.

Frederick Danker has found a different model for understanding Luke's christology. In his book, *Benefactor*, he lays out the evidence for a proposal that is described more succinctly in one chapter of his volume, *Luke*, in the Proclamation Commentaries.[7] In an enormous survey of documents from the Greco-Roman world, Danker pieces together a picture of exceptional persons who were considered to be Hellenistic benefactors. The noun "benefactor," which is used of Jesus in Acts 10:38, is virtually synonymous with "savior" in these documents, and both are used with reference to Roman emperors and other public figures. In Luke's own lifetime, for example, Nero was called "Savior and Benefactor of the world."

The decrees and inscriptions that praise such benefactors make it clear how they are to be regarded. The benefactors are a gift from Providence, though sometimes they are themselves divine. Their coming is good news for the world and benefits all humanity. They are distinguished for word and deed, for both saying and doing what is right. Chief among their contributions are the bestowal of peace and, when a conquest has been won, the granting of clemency or mercy to former enemies. Frequently, the descriptions of these benefactors include references to the dangers and trials they have suffered on behalf of their people. Those who endured death became special subjects for poetic and oratorical exposition.

Luke is aware of the language of Roman decrees, as the prologues to his two works attest, and, in one place, he records Jesus as saying, "Those who have authority over the nations like to have themselves called benefactors" (22:24–26). It is in contrast to these so-called benefactors that Luke presents his portrait of Jesus. In one sense, Jesus is himself the supreme benefaction of God the Savior (1:47). In another, he is the Great Benefactor whose very name is the Semitic equivalent of the Greek word for Savior. Luke emphasizes all of the traditional benefactor elements in his portrait of Jesus: the congruence of word and deed (24:19; Acts 1:1), the bestowal of peace (1:79; 2:14, 29), and the forgiveness of enemies (23:34; 24:47). Jesus goes about doing good, as a servant, healing all who are in need. He suffers many trials (22:28) and is eventually put to death unjustly. Luke's readers would understand such a portrait, Danker affirms, because it was steeped in the imagery of Hellenistic benefactors that was familiar to them.

Jesus, however, is different from other benefactors. He is vindicated after death and continues to offer his benefits through "delegate benefactors," who share in both his power and his trials. By virtue of his unique status, Luke can say that the name of Jesus rates above all others. Jesus is the only one who can offer God's greatest gift of salvation (Acts 4:12).

## Models from the Old Testament

It is not enough to consider Luke's Jesus in light of the Greco-Roman world. Another approach has tried to understand the evangelist's christology against the background of his own Scriptures, the Old Testament, to which his Gospel makes frequent reference.

Some scholars have proposed that Luke employs a "proof from prophecy" scheme in his Gospel, by which he cites Old Testament passages as proof texts in order to establish that Jesus is the Christ.[8] This view, widespread in the 1950's and '60's was largely discounted in a classic study on Luke's use of the Old Testament by Martin Rese.[9] Rese demonstrated that Luke uses the Old Testament primarily to interpret events, to explain their meaning and to indicate that they have divine significance. Unlike Matthew, Luke is not particularly interested in the theological categories of prophecy and fulfillment.

A recent study by Darrell Bock challenges part of Rese's thesis.[10] In his book, *Proclamation From Prophecy and Pattern*, Bock agrees that Luke does not employ an apologetic "proof from prophecy" motif. He questions, however, whether Luke uses the Old Testament to interpret events without reference to prophecy and fulfillment. Luke does not cite Old Testament prophecies in order to prove Jesus is the Christ, but he does use Old Testament references to proclaim that Jesus fulfills ancient hopes and promises.

Furthermore, Bock believes that Luke's use of the Old Testament follows a deliberate progression. First, in the early portions of his Gospel, he stresses that Jesus fulfills the national hope for a regal Davidic Messiah (1:32–35, 68–71, 79; 2:4, 11). To this, he adds a portrait of the Servant drawn from key passages in Isaiah (2:29–32, 34–45; 4:17–19). Accordingly, the foundational christological category for Luke is that of Messiah-Servant, and it is in light of this that the references to Jesus as Son of God should also be considered: the heavenly declarations at his baptism (3:22) and transfiguration (9:35) allude to Psalm 2:7 and Isaiah 42:1 to present Jesus in fulfillment of the Messiah-Servant theme.

After the transfiguration, however, a new theme is introduced. The next three references to Old Testament christological texts (13:35; 19:38; 20:17) all appeal to Psalm 118, a text that has eschatological overtones not present in the royal psalms and servant songs cited earlier. The next important passage (20:42–43) introduces a reference to Psalm 110 in a way that suggests the Christ is not only David's son, but also his Lord. Thus Luke introduces tension into his Old Testament portrait of Jesus, tension that suggests fulfillment of the Messiah-Servant expectations is not the whole story. This tension is also seen in 21:27, where Luke draws on Daniel 7 to proclaim Jesus as the supernatural Son of Man.

In short, Luke begins his Gospel with a consistent portrayal of Jesus as the Messiah-Servant figure promised in the Old Testament, but, by gradually drawing on other Old Testament texts, suggests he is something else as well. Bock believes Luke is content to leave this tension unresolved in his Gospel. In the book of Acts, however, all becomes clear: Jesus is declared to be Lord as well as Messiah (2:21, 34–36). In keeping with Psalm 110:1, he is exalted to the right hand of God, where he is recognized as the glorious Son of Man (7:55–59). He is proclaimed as "Lord of all" (10:36) and "Judge of the living and the dead" (10:42).

What this analysis of Luke's "Old Testament christology" suggests is that, ultimately, "Lord" is the supreme christological concept for Luke. As Lord, Jesus is understood to exercise divine prerogatives and function as the unique mediator of God's salvation. Luke develops this view cautiously, however, by beginning with the foundational view that Jesus fulfills the Old Testament portrait of Messiah-Servant and then introducing passages that describe a "more than Messiah" figure.

### The Meaning of Jesus' Death

All of the models discussed above focus primarily on the meaning of Jesus' *life* as reported in the Gospel of Luke. There has been less scholarly discussion as to the meaning of Jesus' *death*. Indeed, a recent book entitled *The Death of Jesus in Luke-Acts* states that Luke "seems uninterested in piercing through to an understanding of the theological reason for the death or in analyzing what it was intended to accomplish."[11] This is quite a contrast from the approach of writers like Mark and Paul, for whom Jesus' death on the cross is the starting point for theological reflection.

Luke's apparent disinterest in the cross can be seen in the fact that he links God's gift of salvation variously to Jesus' birth (2:11), his life and ministry (19:9–10), and his exaltation (Acts 5:31), but never to his death. The missionary speeches in Acts seem to treat Jesus' death not as the accomplishment of salvation but as a potential obstacle to its accomplishment that is subsequently overcome. Luke omits Jesus' reference to giving his life as "a ransom for many" (22:25–27; cf. Mark 10:42–45). Nevertheless, he insists that Jesus' death is necessary, that it is part of God's plan (9:22, 44; 24:7, 26, 44). What, then, does it mean?

Some scholars have suggested that, while Jesus' death does not have soteriological significance for Luke, it is important for other reasons. For one thing, it serves a moral purpose, portraying Jesus as the exemplary martyr whom persecuted Christians should imitate.[12] In addition, it is inspirational, intended to evoke sympathy for the suffering Christ and facilitate conversion to his cause.[13] Evidence for the first view is drawn from the observation that Jesus' passion serves as a model for the story of Stephen's martyrdom in Acts 7. The second point is substantiated by Luke's unique report that those who witnessed the crucifixion were so moved that they returned home beating their breasts in repentance (23:48).

Recently, there have been attempts to show that Jesus' death does have salvific value in Luke's Gospel, even though it is not conceived of as an expiation for sin. Two different models have been tried, one that views martyrdom itself as redemptive, and another that interprets Jesus' death in Luke as the foiled temptation of a "new Adam."

It is taken for granted that Luke presents Jesus' death as a pious martyrdom.[14] Some scholars have pointed out, however, that in the Judaism of Luke's day, a martyr's death could be considered redemptive. The martyr dies for the sake of others and makes it easier for them to follow where he has gone.[15] Robert Karris has taken up this theme afresh in *Luke: Artist and Theologian*.[16] According to Luke, only God can save from sin and death, but God uses the death of the innocent Jesus to do so. Jesus' passion presents a "double test case" for the integrity of Jesus, the persecuted one, and for the fidelity of God. By remaining faithful in death, Jesus demonstrates his righteousness and awakens faith in those who see him as the innocent suffering righteous one (23:40–42, 47–48). God demonstrates his fidelity by raising Jesus, who typifies God's creation held in the power of sin and death. It is ultimately the faithfulness of God that is the basis of salvation for Luke, and Jesus, as a "model of faith," opens the way to trust in this faithfulness.

Jerome Neyrey also believes the faith of Jesus is the key to understanding the meaning of his death in Luke, but he emphasizes that this faith serves as more than just a model of trust.[17] In his study of *The Passion According to Luke*, Neyrey proposes that Luke ascribes soteriological significance to the faith and obedience of Jesus through an implicit presentation of Jesus as the "new Adam." The view that Jesus abrogates the effects of the first Adam's sin and implements a new creation is found in the writings of Paul and in the letter to the Hebrews. In both cases, emphasis is given to the obedience, faith and righteousness of Jesus.[18] These same themes prevail in Luke's presentation of the passion (22:42; 23:46–47).

Luke presents Jesus as the new Adam in that he is the founder of a new period of history. This is brought out in

the juxtaposition of the baptism and the genealogy peri-
copes, which identify, respectively, both Jesus and Adam
as God's sons (3:22, 38). Adam, however, is not ultimately
known as God's son because of his sin and disobedience,
and so the appropriateness of this term for Jesus must also
be tested. Like Adam, Jesus is tempted by Satan, in the wil-
derness (4:1–13), in the garden of Gethsemane (22:39–46),
and finally on the cross (23:32–49), but, unlike Adam, Jesus
remains obedient (22:42) and faithful (23:46). Accordingly,
the realm of paradise that was closed after Adam's sin is
now reopened and Jesus is able to promise repentant sinners that they will have a place there (23:43).

Neyrey, then, believes that Jesus' death does have soteriological significance for Luke even though he does not
present it as an expiation, a ransom, or a sacrifice for sins.
Jesus' acceptance of death in faith and in obedience to
God's will is the culmination of a radical holiness that has
characterized his entire life. As the new Adam who does not
succumb to temptation, Jesus initiates a new period of history: a time of salvation that may be described as the end
of Satan's reign (10:18) and the inauguration of God's reign
(11:20–22). This is why, in the book of Acts, he can be
referred to as the unique source of life, holiness, and salvation (3:15; 4:12; 5:31).

## The Meaning of Jesus' Resurrection and Ascension

Richard Dillon has contributed a major study of
Luke's resurrection account titled *From Eye-Witnesses to
Ministers of the Word.*[19] After an exhaustive investigation
of the traditions behind Luke's resurrection narrative, Dillon forms conclusions based on the evangelist's redactional
activity. Basically, Dillon finds that the evangelist has combined sayings and narrative material to form a unified com-

position that emphasizes the importance of the resurrection for church mission.[20]

Luke presents the risen Jesus as instructing his followers in a way that dispels their confusion and blindness and brings them to Easter faith. There are two significant points here. First, it is not the historical facts of the empty tomb or the resurrection appearances that bring about this faith, but the words of the risen Jesus. Second, the lifting of the veil is experienced as a pure gift made possible by the teaching and activity of the risen Lord.

Accordingly, Dillon takes issue with those who think Luke's main interest is to ensure the historicity of the resurrection and to establish the apostles as guarantors of the historical fact.[21] Rather, Luke makes it clear that the facts are incomprehensible even to these eyewitnesses until the Lord's revealing word transforms them. As such, they will witness primarily to an Easter faith that proclaims the pure gift of God. Just as the revelation comes to them *sola gratia*, so the content of that revelation is a message of divine grace and forgiveness. The resurrection of Jesus not only undoes the work of those who rejected him but also facilitates the declaration that they are forgiven.

Jesus tells his disciples that it was necessary for the Christ to die and be raised so that "repentance and forgiveness of sins might be preached in his name" (24:47). In this way, the instruction of the risen Lord reveals the positive value not only of the resurrection but also of the passion. For Luke, the traditions of the rejection and murder of Jesus display not the irredeemable perversity of humanity but the invincible persistence of divine forgiveness. Before the resurrection, Jesus' disciples were completely in the dark as to the meaning of his passion predictions (9:45; 18:34). In the Easter stories, however, they come to understand what only the risen Christ could reveal: where human failure is total, God rules most powerfully.

What is disclosed to the disciples through divine revelation will be the hallmark of the church's mission. God responds to human rebellion with renewed grace and continues to offer forgiveness even to those who reject the harbingers of forgiveness. Luke's story of Jesus' resurrection shows the divine purpose most triumphant at the very point where people's rejection is most dramatic.

Luke, however, does not conclude his Gospel with stories of the resurrection, but, rather, with a story of Jesus' ascension. Gerhard Lohfink, in his monograph, *Die Himmelfahrt Jesu* identifies this story as expressive of a tradition that is uniquely Lukan.[22] Although some New Testament passages apparently assume the idea of an ascension (John 6:62; 20:17; Eph 4:8–10; 1 Tim 3:16), it is only Luke who reports the event, and he gives two separate descriptions at that! (Cf. 24:50–53; Acts 1:6–11.) Lohfink also observes that, contrary to the other Gospel writers, Luke consistently records the departures of angels and other heavenly personages (1:38; 2:15; 9:33; Acts 10:7; 12:10; cf. Luke 24:31). Accordingly, he feels compelled to recount the departure of the risen Lord rather than simply closing with the latter's final words (cf. Matt 28:20).

Luke's motive for reporting the ascension as an observable event may be attributed, in part, to his interest in history, and, more precisely, to his concept of salvation history. A visible ascension appeals to him because, as a historian, he wants to concretize events that otherwise could become subject to cosmic speculations. By fixing the ascension as an event in space and time, furthermore, he integrates the traditional theme of Christ's elevation into his particular scheme of salvation history. For Luke, the ascension marks the end of one era and the beginning of another. Henceforth, Jesus will be absent, or, at least, he will not be present in the same way that he was before. The two accounts of the ascension in Luke and Acts separate the time of Jesus and the time of the Church.

A recent study by Mikeal Parsons reinforces many of Lohfink's insights from the perspective of "narrative criticism."[23] In *The Departure of Jesus in Luke-Acts*, Parsons illustrates how Luke uses traditional literary devices for "endings" and "beginnings" in his two accounts of the ascension.[24] The version given at the end of his Gospel closes out the work by recalling elements mentioned earlier and resolving major story lines. The mention of Jesus' priestly blessing (cf. 1:23), the disciples' return to Jerusalem (cf. 2:45), and their continuous blessing of God in the Temple (cf. 2:37) all make allusions to situations in the first part of the story. Furthermore, the concluding reference to the disciples in the Temple provides a certain resolution to the conflict that has been developed with regard to that institution throughout the narrative: at the end of Luke's story, the Temple is at last a "cleansed house" (cf. 19:45–48). When the resurrection and ascension stories in chapter 24 are taken together as a unit, such instances of "closure" are even more numerous, leading Parsons to believe that Luke intends them to be read as the dramatic conclusion to his work. The final image that he wishes to impress upon his readers is that of the disciples, despite the absence of their Lord, blessing God and obeying his commands with joy.

Parsons goes on to analyze the ascension narrative in Acts and finds that it serves the opposite literary purpose of opening rather than closing a work. In fact, the various discrepancies between Luke's two accounts can be accounted for in terms of their literary function: one closes out the Gospel and the other opens the story of Acts.

It would seem, then, that Parsons confirms in his literary study what Lohfink held to be the theological significance of the two accounts: they separate the story of Jesus in the Gospel from that of the Church in Acts. In another sense, however, the two accounts may be considered a bridge between the two books. What Luke wants to emphasize is that the Church provides the ending to the story of Jesus, just as Jesus provides the beginning to the story of the Church.[25] In the final analysis, the literary effect of beginning one book with the same incident that ended another ties the two works together and stresses the continuity rather than the distinctiveness of their contents.

In his study, *Christ the Lord*, Eric Franklin deals with still another aspect of the ascension in Luke, namely the apparent change of status it confers upon Jesus.[26] Before this event, Jesus is presented primarily as one obedient to God, but, afterwards, he becomes himself the object of worship (24:52). In Acts, the disciples pray to him (7:59) and call upon his name (9:13–14). In one key passage, Peter even proclaims that it is through the exaltation that God has made Jesus Lord and Christ (2:32–36).

The change in status is only apparent, however, for Luke makes it clear that Jesus is both Lord and Christ from his birth (2:11). Furthermore, his subordination to the Father does not cease altogether after the exaltation (Acts 4:24–30). What the ascension signifies is the visible and concrete revelation of Jesus' status. It is as much a transition in the apprehension of the disciples as in the career of Jesus, for it is not until this moment that understanding and joy come to them (24:52–53).

As such, the ascension account that ends Luke's Gospel puts the whole volume into perspective and shows its significance. In his first book, Luke concentrates on presenting Jesus as the Christ, a role that is further defined in terms of the Old Testament concepts of "Prophet" and "Servant of God." Like the disciples, however, Luke's reader is compelled by the glorification of Jesus at the ascension to reconsider this presentation. It is then recognized that the life described is that of the one now known as "the Lord." What Luke does in his Gospel, then, is present the earthly life of Jesus in such a way that it can be seen, in retrospect, to congeal with the more explicit christology of Acts. Luke considers Jesus to be the ever-present, exalted Lord who is worshipped by the community. Accordingly, he tells the story of Jesus' life as a movement toward exaltation and as a fitting prelude to the recognition and glorification that he now receives.

## Salvation History and Eschatology

The question of the continuity between Luke's story of Jesus and his story of the Church touches on what has been perhaps the most controversial issue in Lukan scholarship: Luke's view of salvation history and eschatology.

As indicated in Chapter One of this book, Hans Conzelmann set the stage for much future discussion of Luke's Gospel when he proposed that Luke divides history into three distinct periods: the time of Israel, the time of Jesus, and the time of the Church. The break between the first two periods is indicated in 16:16 when Jesus says, "The law and the prophets were until John; since then, the good news of the Kingdom of God is preached." The break between the second and third periods is indicated by the division between the Gospel and Acts and by the latter's unique description of a community that must persevere for an extended period of time in the absence of its Lord.

Conzelmann's identification of the first break in time is generally recognized, although there has been much discussion as to whether Luke intends to place John the Baptist in the first or second period.[27] The second break, however, is more debatable and the ramifications of its acceptance more momentous. By introducing the "time of the Church" as a major era of history and by placing Jesus in "the middle of time," Luke, according to Conzelmann, accepts the delay of the parousia as inevitable and prepares his Church for the long haul. He sacrifices, however, something essential to the eschatological proclamation of the Gospel, namely, the present accessibility of salvation.

Conzelmann claims that, for Luke, salvation was available in the past and it will become available again in the distant future, but, for now, the Church survives on memories and promises. Luke "historicizes" the salvation brought by Christ; he is the only New Testament writer who features the historical Jesus as announcing, "Today salvation has come . . ." (19:9; cf. 2:11; 4:21; 22:43). But for Luke's community, this "today" belongs to the past; it does not carry the immediacy of, say, Paul's proclamation that "*now* is the day of salvation" (2 Cor 6:2). For Luke, the time of salvation is not "now," it is past, and its return at the end of time has been postponed indefinitely. In the meanwhile, the Church may be strengthened through the gift of the Holy Spirit, but it will also have to endure many trials (Acts 14:22).[28]

Conzelmann's thesis found initial wide acceptance and influenced the work of many. Gerhard Schneider wrote that Luke replaces the hope of an imminent parousia with an exhortation to always be ready.[29] Jacques Dupont suggested that he substitutes for the ultimate hope an "individual eschatology," by which salvation is received by the believer at the end of his or her earthly life.[30] Günter Klein observed that the effect of Luke's enterprise is to make reception of salvation dependent upon communion with the sacred past, which is only accessible through legitimate tradition.[31] In one way or another, all these proposals are variations on the basic theme sounded by Conzelmann.

Helmut Flender, in his book *St. Luke: Theologian of Redemptive History*, proposes a somewhat different model.[32] To understand Luke's thinking aright it is necessary to realize that his scheme is influenced by a distinction between earthly and celestial modes of being. Salvation history and eschatology have a vertical as well as horizontal dimension, for the earthly and heavenly spheres exist concurrently. Basically, Luke understands things as working out according to the scheme described in Revelation 12: a victory in heaven first, and then the restoration of all things on earth. From Luke's point of view, the first step is completed and the second is in the process of being fulfilled.

According to Flender, the ascension of Jesus should not be understood negatively, as a departure that precedes a period of absence, but positively, as the inauguration of his present reign. In fact, Luke has transferred many functions usually associated with Christ at his parousia to his exaltation, notably, the outpouring of the Holy Spirit. Observing that Daniel 7:13 did not originally refer to the Son of Man coming to earth but to his enthronement in heaven, Flender affirms that, for Luke, the ascension and the parousia are virtually identified. The day of the Son of Man's revelation on earth (17:30) will be but one of the "days of the Son of Man" (17:22) that have already begun.

It has been said that Flender simply restates Luke's predicament in spatial rather than temporal terms. Whereas Conzelmann sees salvation as removed to the past or future, Flender represents it as removed to the heavens.[33] He insists, however, that salvation remains perpetually present in a dialectical sense. Although Christians continue to live a historical existence, they are not caught in a dismal period of transition. Rather, they enjoy communion with the risen Christ and receive the Holy Spirit, which Flender considers much more than just a "substitute" for genuine salvation. Accordingly, when Christian preachers tell potential converts that God will send Christ to them (Acts 3:20), they are in effect promising a personal parousia to all who repent. Similarly, Jesus' words regarding the "today" of salvation are to be read existentially. Luke intends for his readers to hear the promises of fulfillment and salvation as applicable to their own "today" in a way that transcends the historical sense. The Church, then, shares in the basically changed situation brought about by Jesus while, at the same time, participating in the renewal of the world. This mission takes place under the direction of the heavenly Christ and the guidance of the Spirit. The message of a salvation already completed by Christ transforms the world in a way that prefigures the consummation of that salvation on earth.

## Observations and Conclusions

Though many various ideas concerning Luke's view of Jesus are presented in this chapter, the careful reader will have already noted points of convergence between them. It is widely recognized that the Gospel and Acts present different portraits of Jesus, but most scholars believe that the same christology is behind them and that a reading of the second book is necessary to understand the first. Luke wants to present Jesus as the Messiah, but also as "more than the Messiah." Kingsbury, Bock, and Franklin all indicate ways in which he does this: by the use of confessional titles, Old Testament references, and the story of the ascension, Luke moves beyond reporting the bald facts of Jesus' life to indicate more fully who he is. Similarly, the models from the ancient world that Luke uses to describe Jesus tell only part of the story. Jesus may be likened to the divine philosopher, the mythological immortal, or the Hellenistic benefactor, but, above all else, Luke wants to say that he is unique (Acts 4:12).

It can be said without question that Luke believes Jesus has brought the salvation of God, but just how that salvation was procured and how it is to be received is less certain, Part of the problem is that Luke himself uses cryptic speech, describing what Jesus "accomplished at Jerusalem" as his "exodus" (9:31) and as his "being taken up" (9:51). These expressions could refer to his crucifixion, his resurrection, his ascension, or, and this seems most likely, to all three. Luke has been accused of harboring a "theology of glory" because he puts so little value on the death of Jesus.[34] Though some would contest this outright, others say that what he really does is broaden the locus of salvation:[35] Jesus brings salvation during his earthly life (19:9), in his death (23:43), and after his glorification (Acts 2:21, 38). The "message of salvation" (Acts 13:26) is understood in Luke's day to include the entire contents of his first volume, that is, everything that Jesus did and taught from his birth through his ascension (Acts 1:1). It is only in this sense that one can understand the rather ambiguous promise, "Believe in the Lord Jesus and you will be saved" (Acts 16:31).

Obviously, salvation has a paradoxical quality for Luke. All scholars would agree that Luke sees conditions now as different from what they were before Jesus came. It is also agreed that he recognizes things are not yet what they shall be. The argument turns on which side of this paradox receives the emphasis: some view the evangelist as proclaiming the salvation that is already present, while others emphasize his struggle to come to grips with the reality of what is "not yet." As the leader of the latter camp, Conzelmann has had his day and his ideas continue to be influential. The increasing trend among scholars, however, is to do justice to the continuity that Luke sees between the time of Jesus and the time of the Church and to his recognition that salvation is a present reality for both eras. In fact, many are prepared to dispense with Conzelmann's threefold scheme altogether and to speak only of two periods: a "time of promise" on the one hand, and a "time of fulfillment" or "time of salvation" on the other.[36]

# 5
# Political and Social Issues in Luke's Gospel

In recent years, the topic that has sparked the most interest in Lukan scholarship has been the evangelist's views on political and social issues. A survey of theological journals will reveal that, in the past decade, more space has been devoted to discussion of these matters than has been accorded such traditional subjects as christology, eschatology, and ecclesiology. In part, this may be due to the rise of liberation theology, the development of feminist hermeneutics, and the increased appreciation for the work of scholars in the third world. In another sense, however, the tendency to understand Luke through his politics is not new, for it has long been recognized that this Gospel displays an extraordinary awareness of the world in which it was written. Luke's historical notes (1:5; 2:1–2; 3:1–2) indicate that he intends to tie the significance of the events he reports to their social context. The book of Acts features numerous accounts that prove he is aware of the benefits and hazards that political connections can pose to the Church. It is not surprising, then, that even in the nineteenth century, political motivations were considered important for an understanding of Luke's project.[1] For our purposes, however, the discussion will begin, once more, with Conzelmann.

## A Political Apology

Hans Conzelmann believes one purpose of Luke's work is to present a political apology for Christianity to the Roman empire.[2] The need for this is occasioned by Luke's recognition that the parousia has been delayed indefinitely and the Church may have to co-exist with society for an extended period of time. Luke wants to enter into conversation with the state in hopes of achieving a permanent settlement.

Luke wants to show the Romans that Christianity is politically harmless. In the Gospel, he does this by making it clear that Jesus posed no political threat and that the Roman rulers recognized this (23:4, 14–15, 22). Jesus advocated giving Caesar his due (20:25), just as John the Baptist encouraged good citizenship (3:10–14). These themes continue in the book of Acts, where Christians are able to appeal to Rome for support and are declared innocent of any wrongdoing (18:12–17; 22:23–29; 25:23–27; 26:32). Throughout his defense of Christianity, Luke finds a perfect scapegoat for past trouble in the Jews, who have just waged war with Rome and suffered a humiliating defeat. Luke indicates that all of the problems concerning Jesus and the early Christian missionaries were incited by the Jews, whom the Romans know to be troublemakers.

Conzelmann's thesis is often disputed, but it has been very influential. Charles Giblin, for example, builds on this basic concept when he suggests that, alongside the apology for Christianity, Luke delivers a warning to potential enemies of the faith.[3] He does this by presenting the fate of Jerusalem as a historical-typological moral for his readers. Luke's Gospel interprets the destruction of that city as a judgment from God. Its fate is sealed by its rejection of Jesus and his disciples. Luke expects his reader to ask,

"What will happen to my city (state or society) if we reject Jesus and his messengers?" The moral to be drawn by Gentile rulers is that, if they want to avoid the errors of the Jewish leaders, it will be in their best interest to be receptive to the Christian message.

Another scholar, Paul Walaskay, has attempted to modify Conzelmann's argument while retaining its basic theme.[4] Because he can find no solid evidence to indicate that persecution from Rome was a problem for Luke's community, he suggests that Conzelmann's thesis be turned "upside-down." Instead of defending the Church to the empire, he supposes that Luke is defending the empire to the Church. Luke is decidedly pro-Roman and wants to show the Christians of his day that improved relations with the empire can facilitate the Church's further expansion. Since some may have problems of conscience in coming to terms with the political, social, and cultural context of Rome, he approaches his task as one who initiates a dialogue. He points out certain positive features of Roman rule and reminds his readers that God stands behind all human institutions and delegates authority to them.

Philip Esler uses the term "social legitimation" to describe the political and social motivations of Luke's project.[5] Like Walaskay, he does not believe the evangelist is presenting an appeal on behalf of the Church to those without. He addresses what he has to say about Rome to his own community. He does not offer, however, an apology or defense of the empire for people who need to be convinced of its legitimacy. Rather, Luke wants to reassure Roman Christians of the possibility of joint allegiance to the empire and the faith. In sociological terms, this offers the movement a "legitimation" of the development that has already occurred. Luke emphasizes the Roman declarations of Jesus' innocence because it is important for Roman Christians to know that Jesus did not contravene their law. In short, Luke does not seek to justify Christianity to Rome or to defend Rome to the Church; he provides legitimation of Roman Christianity for the Roman Christians themselves.

Giblin, Walaskay, and Esler all modify or challenge portions of Conzelmann's thesis, but they retain the basic idea that Luke envisions peaceful coexistence between Church and state. Richard Cassidy, on the other hand, completely rejects this premise.[6] In an influential book, *Jesus, Politics, and Society*, he argues that Luke's Gospel could never have been intended as a political apologetic or as an attempt to make peace with the existing social order. For one thing, the words and deeds of Jesus reported in this Gospel are of such revolutionary consequence that no one who reads them would ever be convinced this man was politically harmless. Jesus advocates a new society, one that is based on service and humility rather than traditional power structures (22:24–27). He opposes injustice, speaks out against oppression, advocates nonviolence, affirms new roles for women, condemns the rich, and praises those who give away their possessions. Luke presents Jesus as one who refuses to defer to authorities. He calls Herod a "fox" (12:31–33) and speaks of Pilate's atrocities (13:1–3). He defies the Jewish Sanhedrin (22:67–70) and repudiates Gentile rulers (22:24–27). He also predicts that those who are faithful to him will incur trouble from secular authorities (21:12). In the final analysis, Cassidy decides, Pilate and Herod were wrong in pronouncing Jesus innocent. According to Luke, Jesus ultimately posed more of a threat to the existing social order than their ironic pronouncements took into account.

**A Call to Revolution**

If Richard Cassidy contests the thesis that Luke presents Jesus as politically harmless, it must be asked whether he favors the opposite extreme: does he mean to suggest that Luke presents Jesus as an instigator of revolution? This view is explicitly developed in a work that influenced Cassidy, *Jesus and the Nonviolent Revolution* by André Trocmé.[7] Specifically, Trocmé sees Jesus in Luke as one who tries to revive the ancient Jewish custom of "Jubilee." As described in key Old Testament texts (Lev 25; Ex 21:2–6; 23:10–12; and Dt 15:1–18; 31:9–13), the proclamation of a Jubilee year would imply the following provisions: the land would be allowed to lay fallow for one year, debts would be remitted, slaves would be released, and capital would be redistributed. It is obvious that any attempt to implement such measures in first-century Palestine would instigate a social and political upheaval.

Trocmé believes that this is just what Jesus does, in the Gospel of Luke and elsewhere. The crucial text for this theory is Luke 4:16–32, where, in a programmatic statement, Jesus describes his mission as being "to preach good news to the poor," "to proclaim release to the captives," "to set at liberty those who are oppressed," and "to proclaim the acceptable year of the Lord" (vs. 18–19). Jesus is quoting passages from Isaiah here (Isaiah 61:1–2; 58:6), passages that reflect the Jubilee theme. According to Trocmé, the "favorable year of the Lord" that Jesus proclaims is the Year of Jubilee, and the good news he preaches to the poor can be understood in socio-political terms. In short, Luke presents Jesus as calling for an immediate restructuring of society that will make it impossible for a minority to accumulate capital at the expense of the masses. It is not surprising, then, that the wealthy sabbath-goers who hear his words respond with murderous rage (4:28–29).

The revolutionary theme of Jubilee can be seen at other points in Luke's Gospel, too. It is because the land must be left fallow for a year that Jesus teaches against anxiety over food and drink (12:29–31). The remittance of debts, which implies the liberation of "debt slaves" as well, is referred to in the model prayer Jesus teaches (11:4) and is exemplified in a parable he tells (16:1–13). As for the redistribution of capital, Jesus commands the selling of possessions (12:30–33; 18:22) and insists that mere tithing is not enough (11:42). That these instructions are intended to imply a literal economic restructuring is apparent from the practice of the early Church, as described in Acts (2:44–45; 4:34–35).

Trocmé's ideas about Jesus and the year of Jubilee have been popularized in America through John Howard Yoder's book, *The Politics of Jesus.*[8] Together, these two scholars have contributed greatly to current socio-political interpretations of the New Testament. It must be noted, however, that both Trocmé and Yoder are more interested in the attitude of Jesus than in that of Luke. Though they deal largely with material found in Luke, they do not make use of the scholarly methods that are designed to discern the evangelist's own perspective.

Robert Sloan provides an exegetical analysis of the Lukan Jubilee texts in his book, *The Favorable Year of the Lord.*[9] He discovers that the theme has eschatological and cultic dimensions for Luke that Trocmé and Yoder fail to take into account. Since Luke represents the proclamation of Jubilee as having been fulfilled by the coming of Jesus (4:21), it is unlikely that he understands that proclamation in primarily legal or political terms. The Greek word used in 4:18 to describe the effects of Jesus' ministry as "release" of captives and "liberty" for the oppressed is used elsewhere by Luke for "forgiveness" of sins. Furthermore, Sloan notes that the Isaiah passages to which Jesus refers in Luke 4:18–19 are themselves reinterpretations of the Jubilee theme in new, eschatological contexts. Isaiah 61:1–2 alludes to the Jubilee tradition as a way of expressing Israel's release from captivity in Babylon. In a similar way, Luke uses this theme to describe the gift of salvation that God has made available through Jesus Christ.

This does not mean that Luke "spiritualizes" the theme of Jubilee or strips it of its social and political implications. Luke understands eschatology in two stages, present and future, and the theme of Jubilee applies to both. In regard to the future, Luke draws on the ancient Jubilee traditions to describe the great reversal of fortune that the consummation of God's reign will bring. But Luke also sees the fulfillment of this hope as having already begun in the ministry of Jesus and he expects the Church to continue to live out the implications of this. The revolutionary aspect of the Jubilee theme is not diminished by this understanding. In fact, Sloan claims it is the more literal view of Yoder that limits the proclamation of Jubilee to something that happened only once, during the time of Jesus. By taking into account the full eschatological dimensions of this theme, it can be seen that Luke accepts it as a universal concept. The revolutionary image of Jubilee expresses what the Church continually experiences and proclaims, but also awaits.

Sloan's exegetical study, then, affirms the importance of the Jubilee theme for an understanding of Luke's Gospel: it is present in the programmatic address at Nazareth (4:16–21), it pervades the paradigmatic sermon (6:20–38) and the paradigmatic prayer (11:2–4), and it shapes Luke's version of the great commission (24:27). The primary importance of the theme for Luke, however, is that it provides a descriptive allusion for understanding the nature of God's salvation rather than a historical memory of how Jesus attempted to restructure society.[10]

## A Plea for Peace

As the title of Trocmé's book indicates, even those who understand the Lukan Jesus as a revolutionary figure insist that it is a *nonviolent* revolution he wants to effect. Luke's commitment to pacifism is the subject of a recent study by J. Massyngbaerde Ford called *My Enemy is My Guest.*[11] This book's title is based on a distinctive feature of Luke's Gospel, namely his frequent references to Jesus as one who dines with enemies and outcasts (5:29; 15:1–2; 19:1–10). By sharing table fellowship with people who were normally ostracized, Jesus admits them into a covenantal relationship with himself.

Luke's Gospel encourages pacifism in other ways, too. Jesus shows clemency toward inhospitable Samaritans (9:51–56) and refuses to retaliate when some of his compatriots are slaughtered by Pilate (13:1–9). In some cases, Luke's pacifism can be seen to have influenced his editing of sources. He omits the elements in the parable of the great supper that deal with violent retribution (14:15–24; cf. Mt 22:7, 11–14) and he replaces a story that commends the destruction of unfruitful trees (Mark 11:12–14, 20–21) with one that insists they be given another chance (13:6–9). His account of the Temple cleansing (19:45–46) is also quite restrained (cf. Mk 11:15–19; Mt 21:12–13). Finally, Jesus' love for his enemies becomes a constitutive element of Luke's passion narrative. Here, Jesus is presented as the ideal martyr who, in keeping with his own words (6:27–36), refuses to retaliate even in self-defense. Instead, he heals the servant of those who condemn him (22:51) and prays for his executioners (23:34).

Ford's contention is that the theme of pacifism is a special feature of Luke, one which represents his response to the current events of his day. Shortly before Luke's Gospel was written, Palestine was involved in a catastrophic war with Rome and, even after the fall of Jerusalem, unrest and violent turmoil continued. Luke wants to show the Christians of his day that the peace Christ brings is won through love, forgiveness and acceptance of enemies rather than through military struggle and violence.

Aware that this is a radical concept, he begins his Gospel with material steeped in traditional thought. The infancy narratives are filled with militant imagery. It is the war angel, Gabriel, who appears to Zechariah (1:19) and Mary (1:26), and it is an "army" of angels who announce Christ's birth with imperialistic overtones (2:13–14). The prophecies and songs of praise in the first two chapters indicate that God's people are looking for a divine leader who will win honor for their homeland and render retribution to their enemies. The traditions reflected here show a vibrant trust in God for deliverance and for the establishment of messianic peace. The concept of peace that they reveal, however, is similar to the misguided hope that has just brought Israel into its most recent and destructive war. When Jesus comes on the scene, as an adult, a new concept is introduced. Luke presents him, not as fulfilling the traditional messianic expectations, but as proclaiming love for enemies and offering salvation to sinners. Thus Luke offers his plea for peace with the subtlety and sensitivity of a true literary artist.

It is interesting to compare Ford's understanding of Luke's intention with that of Conzelmann and others. Like Conzelmann, she believes that Luke wants to establish peaceful relations between the Christians of his day and their enemies in Roman society. She does not define this motivation, however, in terms of the Church's self-interest or imply that it means a compromise of principles. Luke's concern for peace is grounded in the theological concept of love for enemies, rather than in some practical program for self-preservation and expansion. The forgiveness and acceptance of enemies is not a means to some other end but is itself the will of God and the way of Christ. Jesus demonstrates in his life and in his death that it is the course to be followed regardless of the outcome. In this sense, though she agrees with Conzelmann that Luke has toned down the political role of Jesus, her understanding of Luke ultimately seems closer to that of Sloan or Trocmé. The pacifism that she believes Luke espouses is itself socially and politically revolutionary.

## A Concern for the Disadvantaged

Another notable characteristic of Luke's Gospel is the special attention it pays to those who are oppressed, excluded or otherwise at a disadvantage in society. The list of such persons is a long one: the poor, the sick, the handicapped, slaves, lepers, shepherds, prostitutes, tax-collectors, Samaritans, Gentiles, foreigners, refugees, children, the elderly, widows, and women in general are often cited as examples. Although the needs of such people vary greatly, commentators have long noted a common denominator that links them in Luke's mind: they are all "underdogs" in the society to which Jesus spoke, the sort of people whom others ignore, neglect, or despise.

Luise Schottroff and Wolfgang Stegemann study Luke's unique development of this theme in their book, *Jesus and the Hope of the Poor*.[12] They believe the evangelist re-interprets the message of the earliest Christian tradition in some distinctive ways. For instance, while early Christian tradition recorded Jesus as saying simply, "I have come to call sinners" (Mark 2:17), Luke feels obliged to add the words, "to repentance" (5:32). Why?

Their conclusion is that the socio-historical situation of Luke is vastly different from that of Jesus and so the traditions must find new avenues of application. The witness of the earliest tradition is that Jesus' movement was composed primarily of poor Jews. His followers included impoverished tax-collectors, sinners, and prostitutes. Jesus told such people that the reign of God was beginning and that they were about to be vindicated. Thus, Jesus initiated a real association of people whose lives were hopeless and established a basis for solidarity among them.

In Luke's day, the situation is different, for the Christian community is no longer comprised mainly of the destitute. In his Gospel, Levi the tax-collector has sufficient means to host a banquet (5:29) and the woman of the streets is able to afford expensive perfume (7:38). Since most of the tax-collectors and prostitutes of Jesus' day were slaves with virtually no resources, Luke's descriptions must be considered anachronistic or at least atypical. In any case, it can be seen that the evangelist does not emphasize the poverty of such persons; rather, the focus has shifted to their status as outcasts, as persons who are despised and excluded (5:30; 7:39). Jesus' friendship with sinners, which in the earliest tradition was simply a reality, becomes in Luke a demonstration by which Jesus protests the injustice of an exclusive society. Luke also introduces a theological interpretation of this association, so that Jesus now favors sinners in order to effect their conversion. In the earliest tradition, Schottroff and Stegemann observe, the call to conversion was directed to the powerful. Jesus proclaimed only the elevation of the lowly, not their need for repentance.

The purpose of Luke's redaction, these authors suggest, is to make the tradition of Jesus' association with outcasts speak to a community of respectable people. In Luke's day, the disadvantaged people he describes in his Gospel are no longer the active agents of the Christian message, but he hopes they will continue to be the objects of the Church's ministry. Social tensions, however, still exist and many members of his Church have a tendency to look down on others, for a variety of reasons. Economic status is one factor, but even the wealthy may be excluded on the basis of professional, ethnic, or class distinctions. Luke, therefore, broadens the concept of "the poor," and going back to the roots of the Christian movement, he describes what happened in a way that contends against all exclusivism. He wants the respectable members of his community to compare their own attitudes with those of Jesus' enemies, whom he consistently portrays as "murmuring" against ministry that involves fellowship with the wrong sort of people (5:30; 15:1; 19:7). He calls, ironically, for acceptance by Christians of those with whom the Christian movement began. He wants Christians to "love their enemies" (6:27) and do good even to those they deem their inferiors (14:12–14). Like the earliest Christian tradition, Luke is still concerned with solidarity, but now it is solidarity between those of divergent social and material circumstances, rather than just among the poor.

## A New Role for Women

Along with its concern for the disadvantaged, Luke's Gospel takes a special interest in the position of women, who could be numbered among the oppressed and excluded of his day. Even a cursory reading of the Gospel reveals that women figure more prominently in this book than anywhere else in the New Testament. They are mentioned more frequently and the roles they play are more significant than in the other Gospels.

Luke seems to have an affinity for parallel references to men and women.[13] The parables that liken the Kingdom of God first to a man planting a seed (13:18–19) and then to a woman working with leaven (13:20–21) are also found in Matthew's Gospel (13:31–33). Other examples, however, are peculiar to Luke: the annunciations to Zechariah (1:5–25) and to Mary (1:26–38), the prophecies of Simeon (2:25–35) and Anna (2:36–38), the sabbath healings of a woman (13:10–17) and a man (14:1–6), the stories about a man who lost a sheep (15:3–7) and a woman who lost a coin (15:8–10), the references to two men in bed (17:34) and two women at the mill (17:35), and so on. Significantly, the evangelist also balances his traditional listing of Jesus' male disciples (6:12–16) with a unique list of women who followed Jesus (8:1–3).

It is generally assumed that Luke's purpose in giving such prominence to women is to emphasize the inclusive nature of Christ's ministry and strike a blow for equality. Recently, however, some scholars have argued that Luke does not really intend to further the cause of women.[14] In *Women and Ministry in the New Testament*, Elisabeth Tetlow argues that the evangelist is reacting negatively to the active roles of women in his community and suggesting roles that seem more proper.[15] She notes, for instance, that the women disciples are described as providing for the men materially (8:3) but not as exercising any ministry of proclamation. Luke is able to include catechetical material pertaining to women because he believes it is appropriate for them to listen and to learn (10:38–42). They may also exercise a legitimate role through prayer (Acts 21:5) and alms-giving (21:1–4), but, as the book of Acts makes clear, positions of leadership in the Church are for men only. Tetlow believes that Luke's understanding of the status and role of women can be interpreted in three stages, which follow the stages of salvation history outlined by Hans Conzelmann.[16] During the time of Israel, it was possible for women to be examples of faith and to proclaim the word, as is evident from Luke's description of Mary and Elizabeth in his infancy narrative. During the time of Jesus' ministry, however, this role was greatly curtailed and, in the final period of the Church, it is restricted even more. There are some exceptions to this presentation, such as the mention of Priscilla, who instructs a male apostle in Acts 18:26, but Tetlow regards these as basic to the tradition the evangelist received. In general, she believes that Luke wants to suppress the more dominant position given to women in those traditions and reduce their role to a subordinate posture.

Another scholar, Elisabeth Schüssler-Fiorenza, has also argued that Luke's treatment of women is not favorable. In a series of articles and in her influential book, *In Memory of Her*, she employs a method of "feminist critical hermeneutics" to analyze the New Testament's patriarchal version of Christian origins. In regard to Luke's Gospel, she notes that the evangelist adds the word "wives" to the list of family members who sometimes must be left behind by those who follow Jesus (14:26; 18:29; cf. Mt 10:37; Mk 10:29). The impression thus created is that the radical discipleship Jesus demands is only for men.[17] Similarly, Fiorenza favors a controversial interpretation of the Mary and Martha story in 10:38–42. She suggests that Martha, who is rebuked by Jesus in this story, represents women in Luke's community who are leaders of households. Mary, on the other hand, receives praise for her submissive and silent behavior.[18]

The majority of Lukan scholars do not follow Tetlow

and Fiorenza in their suggestion that Luke wants to limit the role of women. Jane Kopas, for example, thinks his portrayal of women suggests a measure of equality that goes well beyond the expectations of his time.[19] Rosalie Ryan disputes the notion that Luke wants to restrict radical discipleship to men, since he refers frequently to the women of Galilee who follow Jesus throughout the Gospel (8:1–3; 23:49, 55; 24:10; cf. Acts 1:14).[20] Against Fiorenza's interpretation of the Mary and Martha pericope, it is often said that Luke portrays Jesus here as challenging the view that a woman's role should be limited to such traditional duties as doing housework and providing hospitality. His defense of Mary, then, does not commend submissiveness so much as it affirms the right of women to learn the word the same as men.[21]

The view that Luke presents women as disciples, and so as models of discipleship, finds its supreme expression in the Gospel's presentation of Mary, the mother of Jesus. An ecumenical task force studying the topic *Mary in the New Testament* recently came to the conclusion that, in Luke's Gospel, Mary is portrayed as the ideal disciple, a figure whom women and men alike should emulate.[22] Her response to the angel, "Let it be to me according to your word" (1:38), marks her as the first Christian disciple. She exemplifies growth as a believer by allowing what she cannot immediately understand to sink into her memory until she is able to work out the meaning (2:19, 51). She is not spared the test of discipleship (2:25), but perseveres to become part of the apostolic community (Acts 1:14). Indeed, Luke's recurring theme concerning Mary is that she embodies what he considers to be constitutive of true discipleship, the hearing and doing of God's word. Elizabeth pronounces her forever blessed because she has believed the Lord's word (1:45). Jesus himself describes her as one who "hears the word of God and keeps it" (8:21; cf. 11:28–29).

Does Luke's choice of a woman as the ideal model for discipleship suggest that he advocates a new role for women in general? One passage has been interpreted as implying that it might. In Luke 11:28–29, a woman from the crowd calls out to Jesus, "Blessed is the womb that bore you and the breasts that gave you suck." This acclaim for his mother reflects the traditional view that women find honor primarily through their attachment to great men or through the bearing of great sons. Jesus, however, overturns this ideology when he responds, "Blessed, rather, are those who hear the word of God and keep it." In short, Luke portrays Jesus as insisting, even in regard to his own mother, that a woman is to be evaluated on the same basis as a man.[23]

## A Message to the Rich and Poor

The social issue in Luke's Gospel that has attracted the most attention over the years is, unquestionably, the evangelist's attitude toward wealth and poverty. The preponderance of scholarly writings on this topic mirrors the abundance of material that Luke himself devotes to it. This Gospel preserves more traditions related to the theme of possessions than any of the others. It is only here, for instance, that one finds the story of Zacchaeus (19:1–10) or the parables of the Rich Fool (12:13–21), the Unjust Steward (16:1–15), and the Rich Man and Lazarus (16:19–31).

Still, if "Luke consistently speaks about possessions," one scholar observes, "he does not speak about possessions consistently."[24] Jesus spends a lot of time talking about the proper use of wealth even though his disciples have supposedly abandoned their earthly belongings to follow him

(5:11, 28; 18:28). It is the poor, not the rich, who are blessed (6:20, 24), but, on the other hand, it is more blessed to give than to receive (Acts 20:35). One man is praised for giving away half of his goods (19:1–10), while another is apparently rejected because he will not give all (18:18–25). Even in the book of Acts, the Jerusalem Church is described as practicing a type of "Christian communism" (2:44–45; 4:32) but there is no indication that this continues in the churches established by Paul. Some years ago, Hans Degenhardt attempted to resolve these discrepancies by proposing that Luke presents two different sets of requirements for two separate groups.[25] The statements demanding renunciation of all possessions are spoken to "disciples," and are therefore intended for the Church leaders of Luke's own day. Jesus' teachings to "the people" or "the crowd," on the other hand, present a less severe ethic that is expected of all Christians. At first appealing, this suggestion has not held up under close scrutiny. For one thing, in the book of Acts, Luke does not limit his use of the word "disciples" to the Church's leadership, but uses it for all Christians (6:7).

Another scholar, Luke Johnson, believes that modern interpreters misread the evangelist's intentions when they look for rules concerning the use of possessions.[26] In his book, *The Literary Function of Possessions in Luke-Acts*, Johnson argues that Luke uses the language of possessions symbolically. Possessions are signs of power and have tremendous metaphorical potential. They often serve as expressions for personal or communal identity. What people do with their possessions is particularly revealing: acquisition, preservation, renunciation, and sharing are all responses that typify different characters and define their role in the story. For example, in the parable of the prodigal son (15:11–32), the division of property symbolizes alienation, while the father's attitude toward his possessions ("all that is mine is yours") expresses the potential for unity. But the most significant function of possessions in Luke's Gospel is that they symbolize people's acceptance or rejection of Jesus. Those who accept Jesus and his ministry are referred to in Luke as "the poor," and their voluntary renunciation of possessions is illustrative of the new identity they receive. By the same token, "the rich" function in Luke's story as those who will not accept Jesus but who, clinging to their possessions, resist the transformation that he brings.

Although Johnson does not rule out the possibility that possessions also have a literal meaning for Luke, he leaves the explication of this to others. One who has taken up the challenge is Walter Pilgrim, who in his book, *Good News to the Poor*, is careful to avoid "spiritualizing" the theme.[27] Johnson, he fears, blunts the sharpness of Luke's social message through his emphasis on symbolism.[28] The poor in Luke include those who are truly poor, socially and economically, and his Gospel is in part addressed to them. Luke assures the poor and needy that God is for them by portraying Jesus as their advocate. He gives them ultimate hope through the promise that, in the future kingdom of God, there will be a great reversal and they will have the things they lack now. But there is more. Luke also points the poor to the community established by Jesus, a community in which they will find compassion and justice even now. Thus, Luke hopes that his Gospel, like the message of Jesus itself, will be received as "good news to the poor" (4:18).

Luke's Gospel also contains a message for the rich, Pilgrim continues, and this insight helps to explain the diversity of its contents. The stories about rich people who lose out on God's salvation (12:13–21; 16:19–31; 18:18–25) are intended to shock the sensibilities of the rich Christians of

Luke's day, and the stories of people who make financial sacrifices (5:11, 27–28; 19:1–10) are intended to inspire them. Pilgrim agrees that Luke does not lay down specific rules for the use of possessions. Rather, he calls for a re-evaluation of the place they should have in a Christian's life. The call, at least, is to responsible stewardship, which includes giving alms (12:33), remitting debts (6:27–36), and using one's wealth to promote fellowship (14:7–24).

Pilgrim's description of Luke's message to the rich follows a trend in recent scholarship to recognize the latter as his targeted audience. The study by Hans Degenhardt discussed above was titled *Evangelist Der Armen*, that is, "Evangelist of the Poor," but Luise Schottroff and Wolfgang Stegemann suggest it would be better to call Luke "the evangelist of the rich."[29] The days when poor, dispossessed peasants comprised the Jesus movement are just a memory for Luke, but a memory that he would like to keep alive as a critique of his own well-to-do community. David Seccombe suggests that Luke might also have people outside the Christian community in mind, namely, wealthy Gentiles who are attracted to Christianity but fear the social and economic losses conversion could bring.[30] Still, Walter Pilgrim's idea is that Luke is addressing the poor as well. The overriding concern, Pilgrim believes, is to foster a community in which rich and poor alike can hear the word of Jesus and respond appropriately.[31]

And what is that response? Does Luke advocate voluntary poverty, asceticism, communism, or simply generosity? The consensus seems to be that Luke's concern over the use of possessions is just that: a concern. He does not have a definite answer. Still, he is quite sure that treasure on earth and treasure in heaven are incompatible (12:33) and he wants every Christian to consider what, therefore, is to be done. Jesus' disciples (5:11, 28), Zacchaeus (19:1–

10), and the Jerusalem Church (Acts 2:44–45; 4:32) provide examples of what some have done, but none of these is made the paradigm for all. Others exemplify the disaster that can befall those who do nothing (12:13–21; 16:19–31; 18:18–25). In short, Luke presents his Church with a problem and a challenge but does not provide a specific agenda for its resolution.

## Observations and Conclusions

It is easy to see why Luke's treatment of political and social issues has attracted so much attention. The topics discussed in this chapter are still widely debated today and the relevance of Luke's message seems at times uncanny.

The question inevitably arises as to whether Luke preserves the attitude of Jesus on these matters. Although some scholars, like Trocmé and Yoder have used this material as a guide to Jesus' own political views, most have thought it essential to make a distinction between the very different social circumstances of Jesus and Luke. Conzelmann sees the evangelist as trying to tone down the political aspects of Jesus' mission in the interests of current Church/state relations. Tetlow and Fiorenza think he also suppresses the active role assigned to women in the original movement. Others believe Luke struggles to preserve the essence of Jesus' message in a new context: a message originally addressed to the poor and despised must now be interpreted for the rich and respectable. Opinions vary, then, as to whether Luke preserves the radical focus of Jesus' message or distorts it, but it is agreed that he attempts to translate that message to fit a new and broader context.

The question also arises as to how literal Luke's thinking on social matters should be taken. Sloan regards the

Jubilee proclamation as an eschatological allusion and Johnson suggests that all the talk about possessions has metaphorical value. Most scholars, it has been seen, think that Luke is more interested in issues and principles than in specific political programs. He does not, for example, seem to endorse any particular social or economic system to the exclusion of others. This breadth of focus, while allowing confusion and disagreement among his commentators, may be the very factor that keeps his message relevant today.

# 6
# Spiritual and Pastoral Concerns in the Gospel of Luke

In Chapter One of this book, three models for understanding Luke were suggested: historian, theologian, and literary artist. Now it is time to suggest another. Whatever else Luke may be, he is certainly also "a pastor." Throughout his two works, he evinces concern for the spiritual well-being of Christians. He wants to guide Christians into the quality of life that he believes they should experience. In subtle, and sometimes not-so-subtle ways, he offers advice, encouragement, support, and correction.

This chapter will examine some of the "pastoral concerns" that surface in Luke's writings and will take note of how some scholars describe the treatment of these concerns in his Gospel. In general, these are not the matters that have attracted the greatest amount of attention in Lukan studies. At times, there is little to debate: all that is required is to observe the presence of a given theme. Doing so, nevertheless, is a worthwhile endeavor. Any view of Luke that ignores this side of him will be woefully incomplete.

## Discipleship

Charles Talbert has contributed an important study on Luke's concept of discipleship to Fernando Segovia's book

*Discipleship in the New Testament.*[1] He notes that the post-Easter situation of Christians described in Acts is also foreshadowed in Luke's Gospel, so that it is by considering these two works together that one can best understand the evangelist's message.

Discipleship consists, first of all, in being molded by the tradition about Jesus. Talbert believes the genre of Luke-Acts itself testifies to this. He finds the two-volume work similar to certain Hellenistic biographies, which emphasized not only the life and values of a particular philosopher, but also the emulation of that philosopher by his followers. Luke stresses the latter point all the more by structuring his two books according to parallel literary patterns. Remarkable correspondences can be discerned between what Jesus says and does in Luke and what the disciples say and do in Acts. Thus, Luke intends to graphically illustrate how Christians who live after Easter should take the earthly Jesus as their model. Luke records this Jesus as saying, "A disciple is not above his teacher, but every one who is fully taught will be like his teacher" (6:40). For Luke, discipleship consists largely of following the example of Jesus as recorded in the tradition about him.

There is more to being a Christian, however, than simply patterning one's life after that of Jesus. In Luke's view, disciples must be enabled to follow Jesus by experiencing his call (5:1–11, 27–28; cf. Acts 9:1–31). Furthermore, disciples are not solitary individuals but participants in community. This dimension of the Christian life is emphasized throughout Acts, and it is also foreshadowed in the Gospel through the corporate life of Jesus' disciples (8:1–3; 9:1–6; 10:1–24; 22:28–30).

Talbert emphasizes further that Luke's concept of discipleship applies not only to the way Christians are to live but also to the mission they are to fulfill. This mission, of course, is also shaped by the tradition about Jesus, for an integral part of that tradition is that Jesus commissioned his disciples to be witnesses (5:1-11; 24:46-49). Luke also records two stories in which Jesus sends the disciples out as missionaries (9:1-6; 10:1-24). These stories are particularly enlightening, for they emphasize both that the disciples are empowered by Jesus for the mission they are to fulfill (9:1) and that they are to undertake this mission in partnership with others (10:1). Luke's concept of mission, therefore, corresponds closely to his concept of the Christian way of life. In both cases, discipleship consists of being molded by a tradition, being empowered by an experience, and being participants in a community.

Talbert concludes that Luke has a balanced, wholistic view of discipleship. Discipleship consists equally of emulating the example of Jesus and being enabled by an ongoing experience of his power. It is based on Christian tradition and grounded in Christian community, but is also lived out in mission to the world. It is only by holding all of these components together that the distinctively Lukan view of discipleship can be maintained.

### The Word of Salvation

In his book, *Jesus Christ in Matthew, Mark and Luke*, Jack Kingsbury draws some interesting comparisons between four early Christian witnesses: the three Synoptic Gospels and Q.[2] The Gospel of Mark, Kingsbury says, locates salvation in Jesus' death on the cross, while the Q source located it in the parousia. For the Gospel of Matthew, the locus of salvation is found in the Church, in the presence of the exalted Son of God with his people. What about Luke? For Luke, Kingsbury decides, salvation is found in the word about Jesus, the word that is proclaimed by the Church.

This is the case, for example, in the book of Acts. In

numerous incidents, the word about Jesus is proclaimed and those who believe this word repent and are baptized. By so doing, they become members of the Church, and they receive forgiveness of sins and the gift of the Holy Spirit. In short, they are saved. A closer look at what is said when the word is proclaimed in Acts reveals that these speeches are essentially a retelling of the Gospel in miniature.[3] Luke does not just focus on the cross or on the parousia, but makes the entire life of Jesus the object of proclamation: it is the tradition of Jesus' birth, ministry, suffering, death, resurrection, ascension, and parousia, all taken together, that constitutes the word of salvation.

Since Luke regards the tradition about Jesus as the word that leads people to salvation, it is not surprising to find that he is especially interested in the reliability of that tradition. Schuyler Brown's book on this subject, *Apostasy and Perseverance in the Theology of Luke*, has already been discussed in Chapter Three of this book. Brown's thesis is that Luke's main concern in regard to the tribulations and persecutions the Church has faced is to establish that the tradition has been faithfully preserved throughout. Luke assures his readers that his Gospel is based on the testimony of eyewitnesses (1:2) and of people who were presented with "many proofs" (Acts 1:3). He omits any reference to the disciples forsaking Jesus (cf. Mk 14:27, 50) because this could cast aspersions on the veracity of the tradition preserved by them. He even interprets Peter's denial in such a way that it does not constitute a failure of faith (22:31–34). Thus, Luke wants to give his readers assurance concerning the reliability of the tradition on which their hope of salvation is based (1:4).

The question is how far Luke goes in doing this. Some scholars, such as Ernst Käsemann, believe he goes too far.[4] For Luke, he infers, salvation has come to depend on the bearers of tradition as much as on the word of the tradition itself. Käsemann views Luke as a representative of "early Catholicism," for whom proclamation of the saving word of the Gospel has given way to a concern for preservation of officially sanctioned doctrine. Luke's concern with tradition is to establish a legitimate succession of authority by which one may identify the Church as an institution authorized to dispense salvation. Käsemann believes this attention to tradition represents a falling away from the authentic Gospel and suggests that it warrants a critique from the Pauline perspective of justification by faith.

Many scholars believe Käsemann exaggerates Luke's concern. Eduard Schweizer, for instance, finds no evidence in his study on *Church Order in the New Testament* for apostolic succession in Luke-Acts.[5] Rather, Luke defines apostles as witnesses who were present from the time of John's baptism through the ascension (Acts 1:21–22), and, therefore, they can have no successors. Judas is replaced after his death (Acts 1:15–26), but the practice of replacing the twelve does not continue when others meet their demise (Acts 12:1–2). In fact, the apostles soon fade into the background in the book of Acts and there is subsequently no unique or uniform hierarchy. James the brother of Jesus obviously has a leadership role, but Luke never tells us just what it is. Paul, of course, is chosen independently by the Lord (Acts 9:1–19). The mention of special office bearers is "almost casual": Luke knows of elders and prophets and overseers, but the prescribed functions or hierarchical standings of these positions are never disclosed. In general, Schweizer concludes, Luke is more interested in the newness of what God is doing in the Church than he is in establishing forms for its government.

In conclusion, it may be affirmed, on the basis of Acts, that Luke views the Church as the agent that brings God's

salvation to the world. The Church does this by proclaiming the tradition about Jesus, the tradition on which it is
founded. Luke does betray a certain interest in bringing
"fringe elements" into the Church: this is apparent in his
treatment of Apollos (18:24–28) and the disciples of John
the Baptist (Acts 19:1–7). The general impression, however,
is more of a concern for unity than for uniformity. Luke
wants to assure his readers that the tradition the Church
proclaims is reliable, yet he is also generous in allowing for
the Spirit to work in surprising and unpredictable ways.

## The Holy Spirit

No one can doubt that the role of the Holy Spirit is a
very important theme for Luke. It is, of course, a major feature of the book of Acts, and even in Luke's Gospel the
Spirit receives more stress than in Matthew and Mark
combined.

Many scholars believe Luke emphasizes the Spirit's
involvement in the career of Jesus because he sees this as
paradigmatic of Christian experience. G. W. H. Lampe, for
example, detects an intentional symmetry between the
Spirit-descent on Jesus at his baptism (3:22) and the Spirit-
baptism of the disciples at Pentecost.[6] Shortly after his baptism, Jesus delivers a programmatic speech in Nazareth
and declares, "The Spirit of the Lord is upon me because
he has anointed me to preach good news to the poor"
(4:18). In Acts, the disciples who are filled with the Spirit
continue this ministry of proclaiming the Gospel. In
Lampe's view, the same Spirit that operated in Jesus comes
to be imparted to his followers and they continue his work
on earth.[7] In the case of both Jesus and, subsequently, his
disciples, it is the role of the Spirit to impart power: power
to work miracles and power to preach.

James Dunn believes that Luke describes Jesus' experience at the Jordan as archetypal for Christians in other ways as well.[8] It represents not only his empowering for ministry, but also his entry into the new age; it marks the beginning for him of what would later come to be known as "the Christian life." This life is marked by a new relationship with God and by participation in God's kingdom. According to Dunn, Luke describes Jesus' supernatural birth, including his conception by the Holy Spirit (1:35), in terms that belong entirely to the epoch of Israel. It is his experience of the Spirit at his baptism that inaugurates the new covenant of "sonship." From this point on, Luke presents Jesus as the archetypal Christian, as one who lives "resurrection life" even before the resurrection. For Luke, then, the gift of the Spirit is the gift of "the matrix of Christian life." Even in the Gospel, he portrays this life as something that is begun and sustained by receiving the Spirit.

Lampe and Dunn seem to agree, then, that Luke describes Jesus' relationship to the Spirit as paradigmatic of the experience of later Christians. This notion has been criticized, however, by Max B. Turner, who says such studies present Jesus as "the first Christian in an epoch before others could become Christians."[9] Rather, Turner says, it is Luke's intention to stress unique aspects of the Spirit's work in Jesus. The address at Nazareth (4:16–21) indicates that Jesus is empowered not for a general preaching of the Gospel but for a specific proclamation of messianic liberty. The Spirit's work through Jesus marks him as the eschatological Prophet who inaugurates the new age of salvation, and in this regard he is certainly not paradigmatic. No disciple is ever called to fulfill such a role and Luke never suggests that there will ever be the need or the possibility for any to do so. The point of the parallels between Jesus' ministry in the Gospel and that of the disciples in Acts is not to indicate that the Church has inherited Jesus' anointing, but that Jesus is continuing his redemptive activity in a new way. The ascended Jesus is the one who dispenses the Spirit in Acts, such that the "Spirit of the Lord" that came upon Jesus now becomes the "Spirit of Jesus" (Acts 16:7) directing the ministry of the Church.

This debate as to whether Jesus' experience of the Spirit in Luke is paradigmatic or unique bears some resemblance to the discussion on Luke's concept of salvation history in Chapter Four of this book. Writing long before any of the scholars just discussed, and, for that matter, even before Hans Conzelmann, a scholar named Hans von Baer made some interesting observations in this regard.[10] Baer noted that, in the Gospel, the Holy Spirit does not come upon Jesus' disciples or work through them. Even when it is said that Jesus gives his disciples power (9:1), the Spirit is not mentioned. On the other hand, Luke shows no reluctance in relating the Spirit's activity in such individuals as Elizabeth (1:41), Zechariah (1:67), Simeon (2:27), and John the Baptist (1:15), for to him these are essentially "Old Testament figures." Thus, Luke distinguishes the time of Jesus from both the Old Testament era when the Spirit occasionally inspired selected prophets and from the Christian era when the Spirit is poured out in the Church. During the middle period, the Spirit works only through Jesus, though the latter has much to say about the future, when the Father will give the Holy Spirit to all who ask (11:13; cf. Mt 7:11). The Holy Spirit will protect persecuted Christians and show them how to bear witness to their enemies (12:12). On the other hand, any who blaspheme against the Holy Spirit will not be forgiven (12:10). Jesus' references to the Spirit all apply to a later epoch, to the time following his resurrection and ascension.

It would seem that Baer's study substantiates Turner's

thesis that Luke intends to emphasize the uniqueness of the Spirit's work through Jesus. In actuality, however, Baer goes on to speak of the Holy Spirit as the power that puts God's plan into effect in each epoch and, in this sense, he regards Jesus' experience of the Spirit as parallel to that of the disciples. This classic study, then, can be cited in support of either of the modern views, though Baer himself seemed unaware of any inconsistency. Many scholars today are content to allow a certain amount of tension within Luke's work itself. It is not inconceivable that the evangelist's pastoral interests would lead him to see potential lessons for discipleship in a particular tradition and to accentuate these even if they did not perfectly concur with his overarching theological scheme. In other words, Luke may think that there are aspects of Jesus' spirit-led ministry that Christians should emulate today, even though, from a christological perspective, the spirit-endowment of Jesus is unique. As a pastor, Luke is less interested in developing a doctrine of the Holy Spirit than he is in calling attention to the possibilities and responsibilities that the spirit-filled life entails.

### Christian Community

On the basis of what has already been said in this chapter, it can be affirmed that Luke understands the basis of Christian community to be the tradition about Jesus. In addition, he attributes the source and sustenance of such community to the enabling power of the Holy Spirit. But what is Christian community like? We will examine several aspects that deserve special mention: fellowship, worship and prayer, teaching and mission.

1. *Fellowship.* In the book of Acts, Luke says that "all who believed were together and had all things in common

(2:44) and he describes the early Christians as being "of one heart and soul" (4:32). It has often been said that his picture is somewhat ideal, especially when compared to the less harmonious images that Paul's epistles provide. Luke knows the Church had problems, but according to him, Christians found ways to resolve their differences (Acts 6:1–7; 15:1–35). In general, the impression in Acts is that the Church is "one big, happy family" (but see Acts 15:36–40).

Is this image of Christian fellowship foreshadowed in the Gospel? As indicated above, Charles Talbert believes it is, through Luke's depiction of the corporate life of Jesus' disciples. Other scholars have suggested that another theme that runs throughout the Gospel might be related to this concept, namely, the unusual amount of attention given to meals, banquets, and table fellowship.

It is often noted (sometimes humorously) that in Luke's Gospel, Jesus is "always eating." Robert Karris is struck by the impression that Jesus seems to be always going to a meal, at a meal, or coming from a meal.[11] Banquets and food also feature prominently in his parables and teaching. In all, Luke mentions nineteen such meals and thirteen of these references are peculiar to his Gospel. Furthermore, as if to call attention to the prominence of this food-motif, Luke reports that Jesus' opponents call him a "glutton and a drunkard" (7:34) and criticize him for eating with tax-collectors and sinners (5:30; 15:1–2). In their view, Karris says, Jesus eats too much and he eats with the wrong people.

Modern readers may have difficulty appreciating this theme, Karris continues, unless they realize that in the thought-world of the New Testament, "food is life and the sharing of food is the sharing of life." Thus, Jesus' participation in meals becomes "acted parables" about life and his instructions about eating together pertain in fact to how people should live together.

Jerome Neyrey notes distinctive characteristics of meals in Luke that help to define this theme more clearly.[12] First, meals in Luke's Gospel are inclusive events. Not only is there the emphasis on Jesus eating with tax-collectors and sinners, but there are also references to Jews eating with Gentiles (4:25–26; cf. 10:7–8) and to ritually clean people eating with those who are considered unclean (14:12–13). Meals also serve as a symbol of election, forgiveness, and eschatological blessing. In some cases, meals provide the actual occasions for conversion (19:5–7) and reconciliation (24:30–35) and, in others, they are promised as a reward for diligent service (12:35–37). On the other hand, meals are also occasions for role reversal, by which the lowly are raised up and the proud are put down (7:36–52). Accordingly, Jesus gives elaborate instructions in Luke's Gospel concerning what on the surface appear to be matters of table etiquette. People should be careful not to shun a legitimate invitation (14:15–24) but neither should they invite others out of self-interest (14:12–14). They should be willing to take the lowest seats rather than the places of honor (14:7–11). They should show proper hospitality (7:44–46) and even those who are leaders should wait on others (22:26–27).

Another writer, John Navone, has noted that banquets in Luke are frequently associated with healing and have a revelatory character.[13] The theme is also sometimes employed negatively, as if to contrast the world's banquet and the heavenly banquet. Jesus tells about the rich man who feasts on the best that the world can offer (16:19–31) and promises only hunger to those who are "filled now" (6:25).

It is easy to see that Luke may be using this recurring

theme of table fellowship to make points regarding the fellowship of Christians in his own day. As the book of Acts reveals, meals remained a primary context for Christian fellowship in the early Church, especially with regard to the eucharistic "breaking of bread" (Acts 2:46). Luke's description of meals in his Gospel, then, may betray his own pastoral interests regarding the nature of such fellowship: he believes it should be inclusive of all elements of society and that it should be marked by voluntary sharing, service, and humility. Healing and revelation should be found here, but not the exclusive and self-centered attitudes that typify associations in the world at large. Finally, the very choice of feasting as a metaphor for Christian fellowship reveals that Luke regards the latter as an occasion of joy and celebration. Christian fellowship provides a foretaste of the eschatological kingdom to come.

2. *Worship and Prayer.* It is only in Luke's Gospel that Jesus' disciples ask him to teach them to pray (11:1). This he does, not only by teaching them a model prayer (11:2–4) but also by his own example and by instructions and exhortations offered throughout the Gospel. Luke's Gospel portrays Jesus at prayer far more often than any of the others: nine times, as compared to five in Mark, three in Matthew, and two in John. Jesus offers three parables on prayer here that are not found anywhere else (11:5–8; 18:1–8, 9–14). He is frequently represented as encouraging his disciples to pray (18:1; 21:36; 22:40). It is not surprising, then, to find scholars who believe one purpose of Luke's Gospel is to teach Christians how to pray.

What is it that he teaches? In an article on "The Prayer-Motif in Luke-Acts," Allison Trites tries to delineate the elements of prayer as Luke presents them.[14] One important feature is, simply, communion with God. Luke depicts Jesus as withdrawing from the multitudes in order to pray (5:16). In one case, this leads to an all-night prayer vigil (6:12) and, in another, such activity is casually described as "his custom" (22:39).

Another important element is petition and intercession. In this regard, Luke is primarily concerned with prayer for spiritual ends. The goals of prayer are to receive the Holy Spirit (11:13; cf. Mt 7:11), to not lose heart (18:1), to escape temptation (22:40, 46; cf. 11:4), and to be ready for the Lord's return (21:36). Intercession for others, as exemplified by Jesus, is so their faith will not fail (22:31–34). Luke emphasizes perseverance in prayer and the need to engage in this activity continuously (11:5–8; 18:1–8; 21:36). He also stresses the relationship between prayer and the working-out of God's plan of salvation history.[15] He calls attention to the fact that prayer is associated with what Trites calls "the red letter days" in the life of Christ. For example, Jesus is shown to be praying at his baptism (3:21) and at his transfiguration (9:28). He prays before choosing the twelve (6:12), before eliciting Peter's confession (9:18), and on the cross itself (23:34, 46). All of these references are peculiar to Luke. Apparently, this evangelist wants to show Christians how God guides people through prayer at every important juncture. Luke does not conceive of prayer as an avenue for attaining one's own desires, but as the means by which God's people may be guided and preserved according to God's own plan.

But there is another essential element of prayer in Luke: worship, praise, and thanksgiving. Prayers of praise have been said to occur more in his writings than in all the rest of the New Testament together. At Jesus' birth, a multitude of angels sing what is now called the *Gloria in Excelsis* (2:14) and the shepherds return from the manger "glorifying and praising God for all that they had heard and seen" (2:20). Such responses are typical in Luke's Gospel and he calls attention to their appropriateness in his story of the Samaritan leper who returns to give thanks (17:11–

18). Luke even regards Jesus' crucifixion as an occasion for "glorifying God" (23:47). Luke's emphasis on praise reflects what has been called his "theology of joy," by which he regards joy to be the "ineluctable goal of Christian living" and the "natural state of one who has found salvation."[16]

Because most of the material on prayer in Luke's Gospel relates to Jesus, the impression might be given that Luke thinks of prayer as a private or individual affair. The book of Acts clears up this potential misconception for it amply treats prayer in terms of its communal dimension, worship. Trites examines the material in Acts also, and finds that the themes sounded in the Gospel recur there. Once again, prayer marks every significant stage in the unfolding of God's plan. And, once again, worship, adoration, and praise typify the life of God's people.

It may be surmised that one reason Luke emphasizes prayer and praise throughout his writings is that, as a pastor, he is interested in worship as an essential aspect of Christian community. His Gospel begins and ends with references to people worshiping (1:8–9; 24:52–53) and it contains more liturgical material than any other New Testament book. Luke conceives of Christians as people who worship and pray together.

3. *Teaching.* In his description of an ideal Christian community in Acts 2:42, Luke mentions all of the aspects of life together that we have examined so far, including fellowship, the sharing of common meals, and prayer. In addition, he mentions another characteristic of the early Christians: "they devoted themselves to the apostles' teaching." This brief summary statement is confirmed throughout the rest of the book of Acts, as groups of Christians are repeatedly described as gathering to hear the teaching of one or another of the Church's leaders.

Although no comprehensive study of this theme has been produced, there is some indication that Luke's recognition of "teaching" as an important aspect of Christian community is evident in his Gospel as well. For example, in the study on Mary discussed in the last chapter, it was seen that Luke presents Jesus' mother as an ideal model of discipleship.[17] Significantly, one of the primary characteristics of Mary in Luke is that she exhibits growth as a believer. She does not immediately understand everything, but she listens willingly and then "keeps" what she hears and "ponders it in her heart" (2:19, 51). Surprisingly, this same characteristic of growth is also attributed to Jesus. Of the Gospel writers, only Luke describes Jesus as one who grows and "increases in wisdom" (2:40, 52). Robert Tannehill has described this as the process of development through which Jesus discovers his mission.[18] The scene of the boy Jesus listening to the teachers in the Temple (2:46) is particularly striking.

It is apparent, then, that Christian growth is important to Luke and that he associates such growth with the ministry of teaching. Jesus' own disciples are perhaps the best examples of this, for the growth that they exhibit between Luke's first and second volumes may in large part be attributed to the teaching Jesus provides at the end of the Gospel (24:27, 45). Their minds are opened (24:45) and they are now able to understand what was previously concealed (9:45). As to the content of the teaching Jesus provides, Luke is very specific: "he interpreted to them in all the Scriptures the things concerning himself." (24:27). We may conclude then, that the teaching that Luke considers to be essential to Christian growth and community is basically an explication of the tradition about Jesus on the basis of Scripture. In fact, this is often what constitutes the teaching of Church leaders reported in Acts, and, at one point, Luke even describes one group of hearers as "more noble" than others because they checked the Scriptures to see whether what they had been told about Jesus was so (Acts 17:11).

There is obviously a close connection between the teaching that Luke wants all Christians to receive and the testimony that he wants them, in turn, to offer others. Richard Dillon has stressed the importance of the teaching Jesus gives his disciples at the end of the Gospel as preparing them to now be ministers of the Word themselves.[19] In short, those who want to be witnesses must first be taught. In Acts, the figure of Apollos is an excellent example of Luke's thinking in this regard. Having received limited instruction in the way of the Lord, he is able to teach accurately about Jesus, but after receiving additional instruction he is able to show from the Scriptures that Jesus is the Christ (Acts 18:24–28).

4. *Mission.* Christian community does not ultimately exist for its own sake. According to Luke, the Church is a community with a mission. Jesus gives his disciples a commission to be "witnesses" (24:48). It is for this that the Holy Spirit empowers them (24:49; Acts 1:8). The work of the Church is to preach repentance and forgiveness of sins in Jesus' name to all nations (24:47; Acts 1:8).

It is not surprising to find that the most important studies on the witness theme in Luke's writings have focused almost entirely on Acts.[20] The book of Acts provides so many and varied examples of what it means to witness for Jesus Christ that it could almost serve as a training guide for evangelism. In fact, this is just what I. H. Marshall thinks it is: one reason Luke wrote Acts was to teach Christians how to be witnesses.[21]

What, then, of the Gospel? Luke's first work, Marshall suggests, provides Christian evangelists with the *content* of their proclamation. Unlike Acts, the Gospel does not provide many examples of what, for Luke, would constitute

Christian witness. The disciples whom Jesus sends out as missionaries preach the same message that Jesus himself proclaims, namely the good news about the kingdom of God (9:2). Although Jesus' followers continue to speak about the kingdom of God in Acts, the central content of their message there focuses on Jesus himself. An explanation as to how such a shift might have taken place is indicated by Acts 17:7, where the preaching of the Christians is summed up as being about "a king, Jesus." Accordingly, Marshall senses a process by which the message of Christian witness came to be less and less about the kingdom *per se*, and more and more about the king, Jesus. Furthermore, because the title "king" was open to politically dangerous misunderstandings, a variety of other titles and concepts came to be used to describe the significance of Jesus.

Taken together, then, Luke's two works complement each other to reveal a pastoral interest in furthering the work of evangelism. It is in the book of Acts that the theme of witness comes to the fore and the task is described. It is the Gospel, however, that provides the message that is to be proclaimed, a message that includes not only Jesus' own preaching, but also the tradition about him.

Luke's Gospel may reflect his concern for mission in another way as well. Not only does it contain the content of Christian proclamation, but it also presents a theological basis for the Church's mission to the world. That basis lies in the concept of servanthood that is presented with such emphasis throughout Luke's first work. Indeed, Luke thinks the Church's mission includes more than just expanding its own membership, more even than just proclaiming the message about Jesus. Christians are called to be servants and are expected to perform acts of love and mercy for others even at expense to themselves.

Luke's Gospel, of course, offers the Church an exemplary portrait of Jesus as the Servant of God. In addition,

Luke helps Christians to understand the meaning of servanthood through his portrayal of the disciples. In the latter
case, the lessons are mostly negative. Still, by showing his
readers what must be overcome, he hopes to guide them
toward acceptance of the servant's role.

Robert Tannehill, in his study of Luke's Gospel as literature, exposes three defects that the disciples exhibit as
characters in this narrative.[22] First, they engage in rivalry
over rank and dispute with each other as to which of them
is the greatest (9:44–45; 22:24–27). The perversity of these
disputes is underscored by their contexts: the first one
comes after Jesus' initial announcement of his passion
(9:44–45) and the second one, at the last supper in the very
shadow of his death (22:24–27). In addition, the disciples
are overly optimistic in that they expect to receive salvation immediately. They believe, first, that the kingdom of
God will appear when Jesus reaches Jerusalem (19:11) and
then, later, that it will be "restored to Israel" after his resurrection (Acts 1:6). Finally, the disciples are unwilling to
face death, a failing that is most clearly seen in Peter's cow-
ardly denial of Jesus (22:54–62).

All of these defects, Tannehill surmises, may be attributed to the disciples' failure to understand the necessity of
Jesus' suffering and rejection. They also fail to grasp his
teaching that "whoever is least is great" (9:48) or to appre-
hend his warning that they should not expect reward or
honor (17:7–10). In general, they are not mission-minded,
but are concerned with their own status and well-being. All
of this changes, however, in the larger scheme of things.
The problems of the disciples that prevent them from being
true servants are overcome after the risen Jesus instructs
them further and provides them with the gift of the Spirit.

In terms of Luke's pastoral interests, then, it may be
said that he hopes, in the Gospel, to inculcate the type of

attitude necessary for Christians to fulfill their mission as witnesses of Christ. By presenting the future leaders of the Church as characters who struggle with the concept of servanthood, he is able to address later believers who may have the same problems. At the same time, by showing the change that ultimately takes place in the first disciples, he shows later believers how they can and should change as well.

## Observations and Conclusions

As a pastor, Luke writes to instruct the Church. He is interested, as Talbert observes, in both the formation of Christians and in their mission. He provides Christians with exhortations and examples intended to aid them in their spiritual growth. At the same time, he challenges them to a discipleship that is lived out in the world. His view of the Christian life involves both joyous celebration and humble service.

All of the subjects discussed in this chapter are treated more explicitly in the book of Acts than in Luke's Gospel. As such, this chapter might provide a transition into the study of Acts for the reader who is so inclined. Any study of the third Gospel must ultimately lead to its sequel, for the evangelist certainly intended these books to be read together. The first book is devoted primarily to telling the story of Jesus and is only secondarily concerned with matters relating to discipleship and the Church. Nevertheless, as we have seen, Luke prepares for the development of these themes in ways that show he is thinking about them even in his first book. His Gospel itself represents the tradition upon which the Church is founded and to which it is called to bear witness before the world.

# Conclusions

If this book had been written twenty-five years ago, around the time when W. C. van Unnik first called Luke-Acts a "storm center in contemporary scholarship," its focus would have been quite different. At that time, there might have been entire chapters devoted to such themes as "Eschatology," "Soteriology," and "Salvation History." These matters are still of interest to scholars today, but they are treated differently and form only a part of the whole spectrum of Lukan studies.

One trend that can be discerned in recent scholarship is a heightened interest in Luke's portrait of Jesus. Today the theological themes mentioned above are usually discussed within the context of christology. Scholars have worked hard to define more clearly Luke's understanding of Jesus and, in so doing, they have provided a new basis for examining his views on salvation and the plan of God.

Another major area of emphasis in recent research has been the question of Luke's purpose in composing his two-volume work. This investigation has attempted to discern the particular circumstances of the evangelist's community and to relate Luke's theological interests to these practical concerns. Conzelmann's identification of the delay of the parousia as the occasion for the Gospel has come to be regarded as too simple an explanation. Other dimensions have also been considered, such as the Church's relationship to Judaism, to the Roman world, and to Gnostic influences. Behind all of this lies the assumption that Luke does not "do theology" in a vacuum, but responds theologically to genuine concerns of real people.

This interest in Luke's social context has been paralleled by a marked increase of studies on his treatment of social and political issues. Luke is, of course, interested in such matters insofar as they affect his own church, but many scholars believe he has commitments here that transcend any particular application. He may be interested in questions of peace, equality, and social justice for their own sake. A number of recent studies have indicated that social and political categories may be as important for understanding this evangelist as the traditional theological ones.

The most important development in Lukan studies in the last twenty-five years has been the diversification of methodology. On the one hand, sociological methods have been employed to uncover insights about Luke's community and to define its role in the development of early Christianity. On the other, various types of literary criticism have examined the genre of Luke's writings, called attention to his rhetorical style, and attempted to read his narrative as a coherent story that is told with particular artistry. These approaches have allowed scholars to look at traditional issues in new ways and have also opened debate on subjects that were scarcely considered before.

Scholarship does make advances. Some students of Luke can still remember when common authorship of the Gospel and Acts was a hot topic for debate, but today there is agreement on this point. On the other hand, a few years ago it was widely held that the "Synoptic problem" had been solved and that any study of Luke could proceed from the assumption that the evangelist had used Mark and Q as sources. The debate on this topic has been re-opened.

What, then, will a book like this look like twenty-five years from now? That, of course, is impossible to predict. But it is reasonable to expect that the focus of scholarship will continue to shift, both in regard to the subjects that are studied and the approaches taken to them. The new methodologies will probably play a big part in the next few decades of Lukan studies, though there is no indication that attention to traditional matters such as redaction criticism and source analysis will diminish. The future will probably see a significant increase in the number of contributions from women theologians and third-world scholars, and these may bring surprising new insights. Scholars no doubt will continue to make significant advances, along with occasional retreats. Some answers will be found and many more questions will be posed. In short, the Gospel According to St. Luke promises to be a fruitful field of study for many years to come.

# Notes

## Introduction

[1]Ernest Renan, *Les Évangiles et la seconde génération Chrétienne.* 14th ed. (Paris: Calman Lévy, 1923), p. 283.

[2]W. C. van Unnik, "Luke-Acts, A Storm Center in Contemporary Scholarship," in *Studies in Luke-Acts,* ed. by Leander Keck and J. Louis Martyn (Philadelphia: Fortress Press, 1980; originally published in 1966).

[3]Charles Talbert suggests that the two books must be read as commentaries on each other in "Discipleship in Luke-Acts," in *Discipleship in the New Testament,* ed. by Fernando F. Segovia (Philadelphia: Fortress Press, 1985), pp. 62–75.

## 1.  Luke: Historian, Theologian, Artist

[1]For descriptions of these and other approaches see Christopher Tuckett, *Reading the New Testament: Methods of Interpretation* (Philadelphia: Fortress Press, 1987); Raymond Collins, *Introduction to the New Testament* (Garden City, NY: Doubleday, 1983).

[2]An excellent survey of attitudes toward Luke as historian can be found in C. K. Barrett, *Luke the Historian in Recent Study* (London: Epworth Press, 1961).

[3]Hans Conzelmann, *The Theology of St. Luke,* 2nd ed. (London: Faber and Faber, Ltd., 1960; German original published in

1957), p. 63, n. 6. A 4th ed. published in 1963 contains material not included in the English translation.

[4]I. H. Marshall, *Luke: Historian and Theologian* (Grand Rapids: Zondervan, 1970).

[5]See note 3.

[6]Charles Talbert, "Shifting Sands: The Recent Study of the Gospel of Luke," in *Interpreting the Gospels*, ed. by James Luther Mays (Philadelphia: Fortress Press, 1981; originally published in 1976), pp. 197–213.

[7]van Unnik, p. 23.

[8]On the other Gospels, see David Rhoads and Donald Michie, *Mark As Story* (Philadelphia: Fortress Press, 1982); Jack Dean Kingsbury, *Matthew As Story*, 2nd ed. (Philadelphia: Fortress Press, 1988); Alan Culpepper, *Anatomy of the Fourth Gospel* (Philadelphia: Fortress Press, 1983).

[9]Robert Karris, *Luke: Artist and Theologian. Luke's Passion Account As Literature*. TI (New York: Paulist Press, 1985).

[10]Jack Dean Kingsbury was the first to describe the Gospels as "kerygmatic stories" in *Jesus Christ in Matthew, Mark, and Luke*. PC (Philadelphia: Fortress Press, 1981).

[11]Karris' treatment of these themes is discussed further in Chapters Four and Six of this book.

[12]Robert Tannehill, *The Narrative Unity of Luke-Acts. A Literary Interpretation. Volume 1: The Gospel According to Luke* (Philadelphia: Fortress Press, 1986).

[13]*Ibid.*, p. 3. The example cited is discussed on page 50.

[14]*Ibid.*

[15]This attitude is often attributed to Conzelmann himself but in fact he refrains from making such a judgment.

[16]See Philipp Vielhauer, "On the 'Paulinism' of Acts," in *Studies in Luke-Acts*, eds. L. E. Keck and J. L. Martyn (Nashville: Abingdon, 1966; German original published in 1950), pp. 35–50; Ernst Käsemann, "The Problem of the Historical Jesus," in *Essays on New Testament Themes* (Philadelphia: Fortress Press, 1982; German original published in 1954), pp. 15–47; "Ministry and Community in the New Testament," also in *Essays on New Testament Themes*, pp. 63-94 (unpublished German original

dated 1949); "The Disciples of John the Baptist," also in *Essays on New Testament Themes,* pp. 136–48 (German original published in 1952); "Paul and Early Catholicism," in *New Testament Questions of Today* (London: SCM Press, 1969; German original published in 1963), pp. 236–51; *Jesus Means Freedom* (Philadelphia: Fortress Press, 1970; German original published in 1968), pp. 116–129.

[17]See W. G. Kümmel, "Current Theological Accusations against Luke," *ANQ* 16 (1975): 131–45 (French original published in 1970); I. H. Marshall, "Early Catholicism in the New Testament," in *New Dimensions in New Testament Studies,* eds. R. N. Longenecker and M. C. Tenney (Grand Rapids: Zondervan, 1974), pp. 217–231; J. H. Elliott, "A Catholic Gospel: Reflections on 'Early Catholicism' in the New Testament," *CBQ* 31 (1969): 213–23.

[18]Cf. *Jesus Means Freedom,* p. 121, and "The Problem of the Historical Jesus," p. 29.

## 2. The Composition of Luke's Gospel

[1]The earliest witness is probably that of the Muratorian Canon, c. 170–80 A.D.

[2]See Jacques Dupont, *The Sources of Acts* (London: Darton, Longman, and Todd, 1964; French original published in 1960), pp. 75–165.

[3]See Vielhauer.

[4]So Ellis, Fitzmyer, and Marshall. Danker is unsure, but says the tradition is not to be "lightly dismissed." Schweizer, however, thinks it "unlikely." See "For Further Reading" in this book for bibliographical information.

[5]It is generally conceded that the so-called "medical language" in Luke is not sufficiently pronounced to establish the author's profession. See Henry J. Cadbury, *The Making of Luke-Acts* (London: SPCK, 1958), pp. 50–51.

[6]For a classic statement of this view, see Vincent Taylor, *Behind the Third Gospel: A Study of the Proto-Luke Hypothesis* (Oxford: Clarendon, 1926).

[7]Support for this view can be found in W. G. Kümmel, *Introduction to the New Testament.* Revised English edition (Nashville: Abingdon, 1975; German original published in 1973), pp. 132–37.

[8]Joseph A. Fitzmyer, *The Gospel According to Luke I-IX.* AB 28 (Garden City, NY: Doubleday, 1981), pp. 92–96.

[9]*Ibid.*, p. 71.

[10]Tim Schramm, *Der Markus Stoff bei Lukas: Eine literarkritische und redaktionsgeschichtliche Untersuchung.* NTSMS 14 (New York: Cambridge University Press, 1971).

[11]An uncertain but possible explanation for this nomenclature is that "Q" is an abbreviation for the German word *Quelle,* which means "source."

[12]*The Formation of Q: Trajectories in Ancient Wisdom Collections.* Studies in Antiquity and Christianity (Philadelphia: Fortress Press, 1987).

[13]Richard Edwards, *A Theology of Q. Eschatology, Prophecy and Wisdom* (Philadelphia: Fortress Press, 1976).

[14]Heinz Tödt, *The Son of Man in the Synoptic Tradition* (Philadelphia: Westminster Press, 1965; German original published in 1959).

[15]Jan Lambrecht, *The Sermon on the Mount: Proclamation and Exhortation.* GNS 14 (Wilmington, DE: Michael Glazier, 1985).

[16]The exact extent of Luke's travel narrative is debated, but these are the limits set by Helmuth Egelkraut, whose work is discussed here. Others suggest the travel narrative ends at 18:14, 19:10, or 19:27.

[17]Helmuth Egelkraut, *Jesus' Mission to Jerusalem: A redaction-critical study of the Travel Narrative in the Gospel of Luke, LK 9:51-19:48.* EH 80 (Frankfurt: Peter Lang, 1976).

[18]9:51, 53; 13:22, 33; 17:11; 18:31; 19:11, 28, 41.

[19]Karl L. Schmidt, *Der Rahmen der Geschichte Jesu. Literarkritische Untersuchungen zur ältesten Jesusüberlieferung* (Berlin: Trowitsch und Sohn, 1919), p. 269.

[20]Conzelmann, p. 65.

[21]P. J. Bernadicou, "Self-Fulfillment According to Luke,"

*BToday* 56 (1971): 505–12; Philip Van Linden, *The Gospel of Luke and Acts.* MBS 10 (Wilmington, DE: Michael Glazier, 1986), pp. 15–37, 143–50.

[22]William R. Farmer, *The Synoptic Problem. A Critical Analysis* (New York: Macmillan, 1964). For a discussion of Farmer's career and an extensive bibliography, see David B. Peabody, "William Reuben Farmer: A Biographical and Bibliographical Essay," in *Jesus, the Gospels, and the Church: essays in honor of William R. Farmer,* ed. by E. P. Sanders (Macon, GA: Mercer University Press, 1987), pp. ix-xxxviii.

[23]B. H. Streeter, *The Four Gospels. A Study of Origins* (New York: Macmillan, 1925), p. 183.

[24]William R. Farmer, "Luke's Use of Matthew: A Christological Inquiry," *PSTJ* 40 (1987): 39–50.

[25]Goulder's book, *Luke: A New Paradigm* (announced for publication by Sheffield Press) did not appear in time for inclusion in this survey. The discussion here is based on his views as stated in the final chapter of *Midrash and Lection in Matthew* (London: SPCK, 1974).

[26]John Drury, *Tradition and Design in Luke's Gospel. A Study of Early Christian Historiography* (London: Darton, Longman, and Todd, 1976).

[27]C. F. Evans, "The Central Section of St. Luke's Gospel," in *Studies in the Gospels: Essays in Honor of R. H. Lightfoot,* ed. by D. E. Nineham (Oxford: Basil Blackwell, 1955), pp. 37–53.

[28]William R. Farmer, "Source Criticism: Some Comments on the Present Situation," *USQR* 42 (1988): 49–57, p. 53.

[29]Talbert, "Shifting Sands," pp. 393–94.

[30]Edwards, pp. 14–18.

[31]Ernst Haenchen coined the term "composition criticism" in *Der Weg Jesu* (Berlin: Töpelmann, 1966). See also, *The Acts of the Apostles* (Philadelphia: Westminster Press, 1971; German original published in 1965).

[32]Jack Dean Kingsbury, *Matthew: Structure, Christology, and Kingdom* (Philadelphia: Fortress Press, 1975).

[33]Joseph B. Tyson, *The Death of Jesus in Luke-Acts* (Columbia, SC: University of South Carolina Press, 1986).

[34]Farmer, "Source Criticism," p. 54.

[35]Conzelmann's *The Theology of St. Luke* is discussed in Chapter One of this book.

[36]Raymond E. Brown, *The Birth of the Messiah. A Commentary on the Infancy Narratives in Matthew and Luke* (Garden City, NY: Doubleday, 1970).

[37]Stephen Farris, *The Hymns of Luke's Infancy Narratives. Their Origin, Meaning, and Significance.* JSNTSS 9 (Sheffield, England: JSOT Press, 1985).

[38]John Drury, *The Parables in the Gospels. History and Allegory* (New York: Crossroad, 1985). See also *Tradition and Design.*

[39]John Donahue, *The Gospel in Parable. Metaphor, Narrative and Theology in the Synoptic Gospels* (Philadelphia: Fortress Press, 1988).

[40]Cf. e.g., A. M. Perry, *The Sources of Luke's Passion Narrative* (Chicago: Chicago University Press, 1920); Vincent Taylor, *The Passion Narrative of St. Luke,* ed. by O. E. Evans. SNTSMS 19 (Cambridge: Cambridge University Press, 1972).

[41]Marion L. Soards, *The Passion According to Luke. The Special Material of Luke 22.* JSNTSS 14 (Sheffield, England: Sheffield Academic Press, 1987).

[42]Frank J. Matera, *Passion Narratives and Gospel Theologies. Interpreting the Synoptics Through Their Passion Stories.* TI (New York: Paulist Press, 1986).

[43]Charles Talbert, *Literary Patterns, Theological Themes, and the Genre of Luke-Acts* (Missoula, MT: Scholars Press, 1974).

[44]James M. Robinson, "The Sayings of Jesus: 'Q'." *DG* 54 (1983): 26–38, p. 28; quoted in Farmer, "Source Criticism," p. 52. Robinson leads the Society of Biblical Literature Seminar on Q, which he founded in 1983.

[45]Farmer, "Source Criticism," p. 52.

## 3. The Concerns of Luke's Community

[1]References are found to Achaia, Boeotia, and Rome. Modern interpreters have suggested Caesarea, Asia Minor, or the Deca-

polis. The only consensus seems to be that it was not written in Palestine.

<sup></sup>²*The Theology of St. Luke.* See the sketch in Chapter One of this book.

³Käsemann, "Historical Jesus," p. 28. Cf. Vielhauer, pp. 45–48.

⁴A. J. Mattill, *Luke and the Last Things: A Perspective for the Understanding of Lukan Thought* (Dillsboro, NC: Western North Carolina Press, 1979).

⁵Mattill follows Weymouth's English translation of the Greek word *mellō.* Some English versions take the word as a reference to the future without any sense of imminence. See Richard Weymouth, *The New Testament in Modern Speech,* ed. by Ernest Hampden-Cook. 3rd ed. (Boston: Pilgrim Press, 1909).

⁶Hans W. Bartsch, *Wachet aber zu jeder Zeit! Entwurf einer Auslegung des Lukasevangeliums* (Hamburg-Bergstedt: Herbert Reich--Evangelischer Verlag, 1963).

⁷Another version of the "two-front" theory is presented by Stephen Wilson in his book *The Gentiles and the Gentile Mission in Luke-Acts* (see note 18). Wilson believes Luke is responding to a renewal of apocalypticism on the one hand and to a view that there would be no parousia at all on the other.

⁸This is the view of I. H. Marshall, who was discussed in Chapter One. See also Oscar Cullmann, *Salvation in History* (New York: Harper and Row, 1967; German original published in 1966).

⁹Kümmel ("Theological Accusations") suggests that Luke acknowledges the delay that has already occurred without expecting it to last much longer. See also Fred O. Francis, "Eschatology and History in Luke-Acts," *JAAR* 37 (1969): 49–63.

¹⁰C. K. Barrett (*Luke the Historian,* pp. 62–66) thinks the grounding of salvation in history is a defense against ahistorical Gnostic tendencies. Georg Braumann and Frieder Schütz think the scheme is the result of a persecuted Church looking to the past for comfort. For Braumann, see "Das Mittel der Zeit Erwägungen zur Theologie des Lukas," *ZNW* 54 (1963): 117–45; for Schütz, *Der Leidende Christus. Die angefochtene Gemeinde und*

*das Christuskerygma der lukanischen Schriften.* BWANT 89 (Stuttgart: W. Kohlhammer, 1969), pp. 91–92. The development of a historical system may also be attributed to the need for definition experienced by the Church when it emerged as an entity distinct from Judaism. See Philip Esler, *Community and Gospel in Luke-Acts. The Social and Political Motivations of Lucan Theology* (Great Britain: Cambridge University Press, 1987).

[11]Charles Talbert, *Luke and the Gnostics. An Examination of the Lucan Purpose* (Nashville: Abingdon, 1966).

[12]Some scholars would prefer to call the ideas to which Talbert refers "pre-Gnostic tendencies," as distinct from the full-blown Gnostic systems of a later period. But Talbert's argument should not be dismissed on the basis of semantics.

[13]See for example 1 Cor 15:12; Col 2:8–9; 1 Tim 4:1–3; 2 Tim 2:18; 1 John 4:1–2; Rev 2:6, 15. The Nicolaitians mentioned in the latter texts continued as a Gnostic sect into the second century; they may be related to the Hellenist Nicholaus mentioned in Acts 6:5.

[14]Talbert finds the same three themes elucidated throughout the book of Acts.

[15]Schuyler Brown, *Apostasy and Perseverance in the Theology of Luke.* AnBib 36 (Rome: Biblical Institute, 1969).

[16]David Tiede, *Prophecy and History in Luke-Acts* (Philadelphia: Fortress Press, 1980).

[17]In addition to the works discussed below, see Joseph Tyson, ed. *Luke-Acts and the Jewish People. Eight Critical Perspectives* (Minneapolis: Augsburg Publishing House, 1988).

[18]Robert Maddox, *The Purpose of Luke-Acts.* SNTW (Edinburgh: T & T Clark, 1985; first published, 1982).

[19]Stephen G. Wilson, *The Gentiles and the Gentile Mission in Luke-Acts.* SNTSMS 23 (Cambridge: Cambridge University Press, 1973).

[20]Stephen G. Wilson, *Luke and the Law.* SNTSMS 50 (Cambridge: Cambridge University Press, 1983).

[21]Wilson thinks the situation had changed by the time Luke wrote Acts. Jewish (or possibly Jewish-Christian) attacks on Paul necessitated an emphasis on the fidelity of early Christians to the law.

²²Jack T. Sanders, *The Jews in Luke-Acts* (Philadelphia: Fortress Press, 1987). Sanders' study should be compared with that of Robert Brawley, which was published at approximately the same time but reaches almost opposite conclusions. Brawley believes that Luke responds apologetically to Jewish antagonism in hopes of effecting a reconciliation. See *Luke-Acts and the Jews: Conflict, Apology and Conciliation*. SBLMS 33 (Atlanta: Scholars Press, 1987).

²³*Ibid.*, p. 317. Sanders cites Ernst Haenchen's oft-repeated observation that "Luke has written the Jews off." See "The Book of Acts as Source Material for the History of Early Christianity," in *Studies in Luke-Acts*, eds. L. E. Keck and J. L. Martyn, p. 278. Haenchen opposes the old "Tübingen school" position put forward by F. C. Baur in the late nineteenth century, according to which Acts was written to effect a reconciliation between Jewish and Gentile Christianity.

²⁴Jacob Jervell, *Luke and the People of God: A New Look at Luke-Acts* (Minneapolis: Augsburg Publishing House, 1972). See also *The Unknown Paul* (Minneapolis: Augsburg Publishing House, 1984).

²⁵Others whom Jervell has influenced include Eric Franklin, *Christ the Lord. A Study in the Purpose and Theology of Luke-Acts* (Philadelphia: Westminster Press, 1975); Donald Juel, *Luke-Acts: The Promise of History* (Atlanta: John Knox Press, 1983); and Robert O'Toole, *The Unity of Luke's Theology: An Analysis of Luke-Acts*, GNS 9 (Wilmington, DE: Michael Glazier, 1984). Joseph Fitzmyer has written his two-volume Anchor Bible commentary on Luke with at least one eye on this perspective. Jervell himself acknowledges a debt to Nils Dahl.

²⁶F. F. Bruce, *The Book of Acts*. NIC (Grand Rapids: Eerdmans, 1954), pp. 17–24; J. C. O'Neil, *The Theology of Acts in Its Historical Setting*. 2nd ed. (London: SPCK, 1970), pp. 172–185.

²⁷A. J. Mattill has argued for a reconsideration of this all-but-forgotten view in a succession of articles too numerous to mention. See bibliography in his *Luke and the Last Things*.

²⁸B. S. Easton, "The Purpose of Acts," in *Early Christianity*,

*the Purpose of Acts, and Other Papers,* ed. by F. C. Grant (Greenwich, CT: Seabury Press, 1954), pp. 31–118.

## 4. Christ and Salvation in the Gospel of Luke

[1]Frederick Danker, *Luke,* 2nd ed. PC (Philadelphia: Fortress Press, 1987), p. 3.

[2]The most important journal articles are listed and summarized in Francois Bovon, *Luke the Theologian: Thirty-three Years of Research (1950-1983)* (Allison Park, PA: Pickwick Publications, 1987), pp. 177–97.

[3]See Chapter One, n. 10.

[4]Talbert, *Literary Patterns.* See also, *What is a Gospel? The Genre of the Canonical Gospels* (Philadelphia: Fortress Press, 1977).

[5]Charles Talbert, "The Concept of Immortals in Mediterranean Antiquity," *JBL* 94 (1975): 419–36.

[6]He indicates that these two models are in fact combined in one ancient work, Philostratus' *Life of Apollonius of Tyana.*

[7]Frederick Danker, *Benefactor: Epigraphic Study of a Graeco-Roman and New Testament Semantic Field* (St. Louis: Clayton Publishing House, 1982); *Luke,* pp. 28–46.

[8]See, for example, Paul Schubert, "The Structure and Significance of Luke 24," in *Neutestamentlich Studien für Rudolf Bultmann,* ed. by W. Eltester. BZNW 21 (Berlin: Alfred Töpelmann, 1954), pp. 165–86. For a summary and critique of the "proof from prophecy" school, see Charles Talbert, "Promise and Fulfillment in Lucan Theology," in *Luke-Acts: New Perspectives from the Society of Biblical Literature Seminar,* ed. by Charles Talbert (New York: Crossroad, 1984), pp. 91–103.

[9]Martin Rese, *Alttestamentliche Motive in der Christologie des Lukas.* SZNT 1 (Gütersloh: Gütersloher Verlagshaus Gerd Mohn, 1969).

[10]Darrell Bock, *Proclamation From Prophecy and Pattern: Lucan Old Testament Christology.* JSNTSS 12 (Great Britain: Sheffield Academic Press, 1987).

[11]See Chapter Two, n. 33.

[12]Martin Dibelius, *From Tradition to Gospel* (New York: Scribner's, 1934), pp. 199–204.

[13]Albert Vanhoye, "Structure et théologie des récits de la Passion dans les Evangiles synoptiques," *NRT* 99 (1967): 135–63.

[14]For a good exposition of this, see Walter E. Pilgrim, "The Death of Jesus in Lukan Soteriology" (Ph.D. diss., Princeton Theological Seminary, 1971).

[15]The classic studies on this view, which tries to find a midpoint between substitutionary and exemplary understandings of the atonement in Luke, are Gerhard Voss, *Die Christologie der Lukanischen Schriften in Grundzügen.* StNeo 2 (Brügge: Desclée de Brouwer, 1965); Gerhard Schneider, *Verleugnung, Verspottung, und Verhör Jesu Nach Lukas 22, 54–71.* SANT 22 (Munich: Kösel, 1969).

[16]See Chapter One, n. 9.

[17]Jerome Neyrey, *The Passion According to Luke: A Redaction Study of Luke's Soteriology* (New York: Paulist Press, 1985).

[18]See, for instance, Rom 3:22, 25–26; 5:12–21; 1 Cor 15:20–22, 42–49; 2 Cor 5:17; Heb 2:17; 3:2, 6; 4:15; 10:5–10.

[19]Richard Dillon, *From Eye-Witnesses to Ministers of the Word. Tradition and Composition in Luke 24.* AnBib 82 (Rome: Biblical Institute, 1978).

[20]A similar theme is sounded by J. M. Guillaume in *Luc interprète des anciennes traditions sur la résurrection de Jésus.* EBib (Paris: Gabalda, 1979). Guillaume holds that Luke's interest is not simply in the Easter message itself, but in the way it is received, assimilated, lived, and transmitted by the community.

[21]For example, Martin Dibelius (p. 15) and Hans Conzelmann (p. 11). In their view, Luke does not intend to offer the content of Christian preaching, but the historical foundation for that content.

[22]Gerhard Lohfink, *Die Himmelfahrt Jesu: Unter-suchungen zu den Himmelfahrts-und Erhöhungstexten bei Lukas* (Munich: Kösel, 1971).

[23]On this methodology, see the section, "Luke the Artist" in Chapter One of this book.

[24]Mikeal Parsons, *The Departure of Jesus in Luke-Acts.* JSNTSS 21 (Great Britain: Sheffield Academic Press, 1987).

[25]Here, Parsons cites Barrett, p. 57.

[26]See Chapter Three, n. 24.

[27]Conzelmann himself places the Baptist in the first era, but many who consider the evidence of the infancy narratives place him in the second or view him as a bridge between the two.

[28]Conzelmann believes that the time of Jesus, by contrast, is represented in Luke as free of the influence of Satan (cf. 4:13; 22:3). Rejection of this point has been widespread, even by those who generally follow his arguments, since the numerous exorcism accounts picture Jesus as doing battle with Satan.

[29]Gerhard Schneider, *Parusiegleichnisse im Lukas-Evangelium.* SB 74 (Stuttgart: Katholisches Bibelwerk, 1975).

[30]Jacques Dupont, "Die individuelle Eschatologie im Lukasevangelium und in der Apostelgeschichte," in *Orientierung an Jesus: Zur Theologie der Synoptiker,* ed. by Paul Hoffmann (Frieburg: Herder, 1973), pp. 37–47.

[31]Günter Klein, *Die zwölf Apostel. Ursprung und Gehalt einer Idee.* FRLANT 77 (Göttingen: Vandenhoeck and Ruprecht, 1961).

[32]Helmut Flender, *St. Luke: Theologian of Redemptive History* (Philadelphia: Fortress Press, 1967; German original published in 1965).

[33]Bovon, p. 253.

[34]Käsemann, "Ministry and Community," p. 92.

[35]Kingsbury, *Jesus Christ in Matthew, Mark and Luke,* p. 126.

[36]See Kümmel, "Theological Accusations," for one example of such a proposal.

## 5.  Political and Social Issues in Luke's Gospel

[1]This was especially true with regard to studies in the book of Acts by members of the Tübingen school (K. Schrader, M. Schneckenburger, E. Zeller) and its opponents (J. Weiss, W. Ramsay). For a discussion of these works, see the introduction to the book by Paul Walaskay listed below (note 4) or the final chapter of Esler, *Community and Gospel.*

[2]*The Theology of St. Luke* (see Chapter One, note 3 above). This idea was advanced in an earlier form by Cadbury, pp. 299–316.

[3]Charles Homer Giblin, *The Destruction of Jerusalem According to Luke's Gospel: A Historical-Typological Moral* (Rome: Biblical Institute, 1985).

[4]Paul Walaskay, '*And So We Came To Rome.' The Political Perspective of St. Luke* (Cambridge: Cambridge University Press, 1983).

[5]*Community and Gospel* (See Chapter Three, note 10 above).

[6]Richard J. Cassidy, *Jesus, Politics, and Society. A Study of Luke's Gospel* (Maryknoll, NY: Orbis, 1978).

[7]André Trocmé, *Jesus and the Non-Violent Revolution* (Scottsdale, PA: Herald Press, 1973; French original published in 1961).

[8]John Howard Yoder, *The Politics of Jesus* (Grand Rapids: Eerdmans, 1972).

[9]Robert Sloan, *The Favorable Year of the Lord* (Austin: Schola Press, 1977).

[10]A recent book by Sharon Ringe explores the meaning of Jubilee images for the early Christian Church and the implications that these images have for theological reflection today. See *Jesus, Liberation, and the Biblical Jubilee: Images for Ethics and Christology* (Philadelphia: Fortress Press, 1985).

[11]J. Massyngbaerde Ford, *My Enemy is My Guest: Jesus and Violence in Luke* (Maryknoll, NY: Orbis, 1984).

[12]Luise Schottroff and Wolfgang Stegemann, *Jesus and the Hope of the Poor* (Maryknoll, NY: Orbis, 1986; German original published in 1978).

[13]Cadbury, p. 234. For more recent lists of such parallels, see Tannehill, pp. 132–35; O'Toole, pp. 118–120; Jane Kopas, "Jesus and Women: Luke's Gospel," *TToday* 42 (1986): 192–202.

[14]In addition to those discussed here, see Elisabeth Moltmann Wendel, *The Women Around Jesus* (New York: Crossroad, 1982), pp. 142–44.

[15]Elisabeth Tetlow, *Women and Ministry in the New Testament* (New York: Paulist Press, 1980).

[16]See the discussion in Chapters One and Four above.

[17]Elisabeth Schüssler Fiorenza, *In Memory of Her. A Feminist*

*Theological Reconstruction of Christian Origins* (New York: Crossroad, 1987; first published in 1983).

[18]Elisabeth Schüssler Fiorenza, "Theological Criteria and Historical Reconstruction: Martha and Mary: Luke 10:38-42," *CHSP* 53 (1987): 1-12; first published in 1986.

[19]See note 13 above.

[20]Rosalie Ryan, "The Women From Galilee and Discipleship in Luke," *BTB* 15 (1985): 56-59. See also Ben Witherington III, "On the Road with Mary Magdalene, Joanna, Susanna, and Other Disciples—Luke 8:1-3," *ZNW* 70 (1979): 243-48.

[21]See, for example, Tannehill, pp. 136-37. For an extended discussion, see the responses following Fiorenza's article in *CHSP* 53 (1987): 13-63. In addition, see J. Brutscheck, *Die Maria-Marta Erzählung. Eine redaktionskritische Untersuchung zu Lk 10, 38-42* (Frankfurt: Peter Hanstein, 1986).

[22]Raymond Brown, Karl P. Donfried, Joseph A. Fitzmyer, and John Reumann, eds., *Mary in the New Testament: A Collaborative Assessment by Protestant and Roman Catholic Scholars* (Philadelphia: Fortress Press; New York: Paulist Press, 1978).

[23]This interpretation is favored by Tannehill, p. 137.

[24]Luke T. Johnson, *Sharing Possessions: Mandate and Symbol of Faith* (Philadelphia: Fortress Press, 1981), p. 13.

[25]Hans Degenhardt, *Lukas. Evangelist der Armen. Besitz und Besitzverzicht in den lukanischen Schiften* (Stuttgart: Katholisches Bibelwerk, 1965).

[26]Luke T. Johnson, *The Literary Function of Possessions in Luke-Acts.* Society of Biblical Literature Dissertation Series 39 (Missoula, MT: Scholar's Press, 1977). See also *Sharing Possessions*.

[27]Walter E. Pilgrim, *Good News to the Poor. Wealth and Poverty in Luke-Acts* (Minneapolis: Augsburg Publishing House, 1981).

[28]*Ibid.*, pp. 177-78, n. 5.

[29]Schottroff and Stegemann, p. 91.

[30]David Seccombe, *Possessions and the Poor in Luke-Acts.* SNTU (Linz, 1982).

[31]On this point, see also Robert Karris, "Poor and Rich: The Lukan *Sitz im Leben*," in *Perspectives on Luke-Acts*, ed. by Charles Talbert (Danville, CA: Association of Baptist Professors of Religion, 1978).

## 6. Spiritual and Pastoral Concerns in the Gospel of Luke

[1]Talbert, "Discipleship in Luke-Acts."
[2]See Chapter One, n. 10 above.
[3]See Acts 2:14–39; 3:12–26; 4:9–12; 5:30–32; 10:34–43; 13:16–38.
[4]Käsemann, "Problem of Historical Jesus;" "Ministry and Community;" "Disciples of John the Baptist;" "Paul and Early Catholicism;" *Jesus Means Freedom*, pp. 116–29.
[5]Eduard Schweizer, *Church Order in the New Testament* (London: SCM Press, 1961), pp. 63–76. Also see Kümmel, "Theological Accusations;" Elliot; Marshall, "Early Catholicism."
[6]G. W. H. Lampe, "The Holy Spirit in the Writings of St. Luke," in *Studies in the Gospels*, ed. by D. E. Nineham, pp. 159–200; *God As Spirit: The Bampton Lectures, 1976* (Oxford: Clarendon, 1977).
[7]On the disciples continuing the work of Jesus, see also Robert F. O'Toole, "Parallels between Jesus and His Disciples in Luke-Acts: A Further Study." *BZ* 27 (1983): 195–212. The same author has devoted a chapter to this subject in *The Unity of Luke's Theology*, referenced above.
[8]James D. G. Dunn, *Baptism in the Holy Spirit: A Re-examination of the New Testament Teaching on the Gift of the Spirit in Relation to Pentecostalism Today* (London: SCM, 1970); *Jesus and the Spirit* (London: SCM, 1975).
[9]M. Max B. Turner, "Jesus and the Spirit in Lucan Perspective." *TB* 32 (1981): 3–42. This particular quote (p. 6) actually refers to the work of Hans von Baer. See also, "The Significance of Receiving the Spirit in Luke-Acts: A Survey of Modern Scholarship." *TJ* 2 (1981): 131–58.

[10]Hans von Baer, *Der heilige Geist in den Lukasschriften* (Stuttgardt: Kohlhammer, 1926).

[11]Karris, *Luke: Artist and Theologian*, pp. 47–78.

[12]Neyrey, *The Passion According to Luke*, pp. 8–11.

[13]John Navone, *Themes of St. Luke* (Rome: Gregorian University Press, 1970), pp. 11–37.

[14]Allison Trites, "The Prayer-Motif in Luke-Acts," in *Perspectives on Luke-Acts*, ed. by Charles H. Talbert, pp. 168–186. See also Wilhelm Ott, *Gebet und Heil: Die Bedeutung der Gebetsparänese in der lukanischen Theologie*. SANT 12 (Munich: Kösel-Verlag, 1965); P. T. O'Brien, "Prayer in Luke-Acts." *TB* 24 (1973): 111–27.

[15]This point is especially stressed by O'Brien.

[16]Paul J. Bernadicou, "The Lucan Theology of Joy." *ScEsp* 25 (1973): 75–98. See also Navone, pp. 71–87; O'Toole, *Unity*, pp. 225–60.

[17]Brown, et al. *Mary in the New Testament*.

[18]Tannehill, pp. 53–60.

[19]Dillon, p. 292.

[20]See e.g., Ernst Nellessen, *Zeugnis für Jesus und das Wort: Exegetische Untersuchungen zum lukanischen Zeugnisbegriff*. BBB 43 (Bonn: Hanstein, 1976).

[21]Marshall, *Luke: Historian and Theologian*, pp. 159–161.

[22]Tannehill, pp. 253–74.

# For Further Reading

Bailey, Kenneth. *Poet and Peasant and Through Peasant Eyes. A Literary-Cultural Approach to the Parables in Luke.* Grand Rapids: Eerdmans, 1983 (Combined edition of works published in 1976, 1980). An analysis of the literary structure of the Lukan parables combined with comments drawn from the author's knowledge of Middle Eastern culture.

Bock, Darrell. *Proclamation From Prophecy and Pattern. Lucan Old Testament Christology.* Journal for the Study of the New Testament Supplement Series 12. Great Britain: Sheffield Academic Press, 1987. Studies Luke's use of the Old Testament in light of his christological interests. See above, pp. 66–68.

Bovon, Francois. *Luke The Theologian: Thirty-Three Years of Research. (1950–1983).* Allison Park, PA: Pickwick Publications, 1987. Translated and updated from French original published in 1978. A detailed survey of Lukan scholarship.

Brawley, Robert L. *Luke-Acts and the Jews: Conflict, Apology, and Conciliation.* Society of Biblical Literature Monograph Series 33. Atlanta: Scholars Press, 1987. Argues that Luke ties Gentile Christianity to Judaism and appeals to Jews to accept it as such.

Brown, Raymond E. *The Birth of the Messiah: A Commen-*

*tary on the Infancy Narratives in Matthew and Luke.* Garden City, NY: Doubleday, 1979. Includes an in-depth study of the background and compositional history of the Lukan infancy stories, as well as a verse-by-verse commentary on the first two chapters of the Gospel. See above, pp. 32–33.

Brown, Schuyler. *Apostasy and Perseverance in the Theology of Luke.* Analecta biblica 36. Rome: Biblical Institute, 1969. Studies Luke's concept of temptation and faith and argues that the evangelist stresses the faithfulness of Jesus' disciples so as to insure a reliable transmission of apostolic tradition. See above, pp. 46–51.

Cadbury, Henry J. *The Making of Luke-Acts.* London: SPCK, 1958. A classic study that treats Luke as an author in his own right and examines the literary process that resulted in his two works.

Cassidy, Richard J. *Jesus, Politics, and Society: A Study of Luke's Gospel.* Maryknoll, NY: Orbis, 1978. Challenges Conzelmann's thesis that Luke's Gospel presents Christianity apologetically to the Roman empire by showing that the political and social stance of Jesus as presented in Luke would be viewed as threatening by Rome. See above, p. 85.

Conzelmann, Hans. *The Theology of St. Luke.* 2nd ed. London: Faber and Faber, Ltd., 1960 (German original, 1957). A classic synthesis of Luke's theology by an outstanding redaction critic, with special focus on salvation history and eschatology. See above, pp. 8–10; 42–45; 76–78; 83–85.

Danker, Frederick W. *Luke.* 2nd ed. Proclamation Commentaries. Philadelphia: Fortress Press, 1987. The standard introduction to Luke's Gospel used by many colleges and seminaries; emphasizes the work's thematic unity and Hellenistic background, with particular attention to christology and ethics. See above, pp. 65–66.

Dawsey, James M. *The Lukan Voice. Confusion and Irony in the Gospel of Luke.* Macon, GA: Mercer University Press, 1988. Suggests that Luke uses the literary device of an "ironic narrator" to create intentional irony in his narrative.

Dillon, Richard J. *From Eye-Witnesses to Ministers of the Word: Tradition and Composition in Luke 24.* Analecta biblica 82. Rome: Biblical Institute, 1978. A thorough exegetical study of the Gospel's final chapter, with emphasis on the "mission focus" of the resurrection/ascension narrative. See above, pp. 71–73.

Drury, John. *Tradition and Design in Luke's Gospel. A Study in Early Christian Historiography.* London: Darton, Longman, and Todd, 1976. An attempt at explaining the composition of Luke's Gospel as a midrash on Mark, the Old Testament, and Matthew, without recourse to the hypothetical Q source. See above, pp. 29–30; 34–35.

Edwards, O. C. *Luke's Story of Jesus.* Philadelphia: Fortress Press, 1981. A delineation of the basic story line of Luke's Gospel, which the author believes can be best understood in terms of fulfillment of prophecy.

Egelkraut, Helmuth L. *Jesus' Mission to Jerusalem: A Redaction Critical Study of the Travel Narrative in the Gospel of Luke, Luke 9:51–19:48.* Europäische Hochschulschriften. Frankfurt: Peter Lang, 1976. A study of the various passages in this central section of Luke and their parallels in the Synoptic tradition, with emphasis on the conflict motif in the Lukan material. See above, pp. 25–27.

Ellis, E. Earle. *Eschatology in Luke.* Facet Books. Philadelphia: Fortress Press, 1972. Presents a two-stage model (present and future) for understanding Luke's concept of eschatology and salvation history.

Esler, Philip. *Community and Gospel in Luke-Acts.* Cambridge: Cambridge University Press, 1987. A study of Luke's community that seeks to combine insights based on sociological research with those of redaction criticism. See above, pp. 84–85.

Farris, Stephen. *The Hymns of Luke's Infancy Narratives. Their Origin, Meaning and Significance.* Journal for the Study of the New Testament Supplement Series 9. Sheffield, England: JSOT Press, 1985. Argues for pre-Lukan, Jewish-Christian origins of the Magnificat, Benedictus, and Nunc Dimittis, which nevertheless anticipate key themes that recur throughout Luke-Acts. See above, pp. 33–34.

Flender, Helmut. *St. Luke: Theologian of Redemptive History.* Philadelphia: Fortress Press, 1967 (German original, 1965). Offers an alternative to Conzelmann's view of salvation history and eschatology in Luke, by proposing that Luke presents the exaltation of Jesus as the consummation of salvation in heaven. See above, pp. 78–79.

Ford, J. Massyngbaerde. *My Enemy is My Guest: Jesus and Violence in Luke.* Maryknoll, NY: Orbis, 1984. Discusses Luke's presentation of Jesus as an advocate of nonviolence, with special consideration of the political circumstances of the evangelist's milieu. See above, pp. 89–91.

Franklin, Eric. *Christ the Lord. A Study in the Purpose and Theology of Luke-Acts.* Philadelphia: Westminster Press, 1975. An overarching study of such matters as Luke's eschatology, christology, and view of the Jews, that tries to situate the evangelist within the mainstream of early Christianity. See above, pp. 75–76.

Giblin, Charles Homer. *The Destruction of Jerusalem According to Luke's Gospel: A Historical-Typological Moral.* Rome: Biblical Institute, 1985. Proposes that Luke understands the fate of Jerusalem as a warning to society as to what can happen to those who reject Jesus. See above, pp. 83–84.

Jervell, Jacob. *Luke and the People of God.* Minneapolis: Augsburg Publishing House, 1972. A collection of essays expounding the author's view that Luke writes primarily for Jewish Christians, addressing their questions about relationships with other Jews and with Gentiles. See above, pp. 56–58.

Johnson, Luke T. *The Literary Function of Possessions in Luke-Acts.* Society of Biblical Literature Dissertation Series 39. Missoula, MT: Scholars Press, 1977. Suggests that Luke's emphasis on the theme of "possessions" has implications that go beyond the literal consideration of how to handle wealth. See above, pp. 98–99.

Juel, Donald. *Luke-Acts: The Promise of History.* Atlanta: John Knox Press, 1983. A general introduction to Luke-Acts that, following Jervell, interprets the two-volume work within the framework of Jewish crisis literature.

Karris, Robert J. *Luke: Artist and Theologian. Luke's Passion Account as Literature.* Theological Inquiries. New York: Paulist Press, 1985. A study of literary motifs in Luke's Gospel and of their fulfillment in the passion narrative; the themes of "faithfulness," "justice," and "food" are emphasized. See above, pp. 11; 70; 112–113.

Kingsbury, Jack Dean. *Jesus Christ in Matthew, Mark and Luke.* Proclamation Commentaries. Philadelphia: Fortress Press, 1981. Describes Luke's unique portrait of Jesus and compares it with the portraits of Jesus offered by Matthew, Mark and Q. See above, pp. 61–63; 105–106.

Maddox, Robert L. *The Purpose of Luke-Acts.* Studies of the New Testament and its World. Edinburgh: T & T Clark, 1985 (first published in 1982). Considers the various theories as to why Luke wrote his two works and decides the best explanation is that he wished to reassure Christians of the validity of their faith in response to Jewish criticisms. See above, pp. 51–52.

Marshall, I. H. *Luke: Historian and Theologian.* Grand Rapids: Zondervan, 1970. Argues that an appreciation for Luke's interest in history is essential to a proper understanding of his theology, especially in regard to his concept of salvation. See above, pp. 6–8; 118–119.

Minear, Paul. *To Heal and To Reveal. The Prophetic Vocation According to Luke.* New York: The Seabury Press, 1976. Focuses on Luke's understanding of Jesus as a prophet and of the disciples as prophets like Jesus.

Navone, John. *Themes of St. Luke.* Rome: Gregorian University Press, 1970. A collection of studies on 20 important topics, such as Conversion, Joy, Prayer, and Witness. See above, pp. 113–114.

Neyrey, Jerome. *The Passion According to Luke: A Redaction Study of Luke's Soteriology.* Theological Inquiries. New York: Paulist Press, 1985. Offers a complete exegetical study of Luke's passion narrative, interpreting the presentation of Jesus as that of a new Adam whose faith is able to save others. See above, pp.70–71; 113–114.

Nuttall, Geoffrey F. *The Moment of Recognition: Luke as Story-Teller.* London: The University of London Athlone, 1978. The published form of a brief lecture that calls attention to Luke's unusual skill at telling a story.

O'Toole, Robert F. *The Unity of Luke's Theology: An Anal-*

*ysis of Luke-Acts.* Good News Studies 9. Wilmington, DE: Michael Glazier, 1984. A popular exposition of major themes in Luke's theology, emphasizing God's offer of salvation in Jesus and the anticipated response of Christians to this.

Parsons, Mikeal. *The Departure of Jesus in Luke-Acts. The Ascension Narratives in Context.* Journal for the Study of the New Testament Supplement Series 21. Great Britain: Sheffield Academic Press, 1987. Offers insights into Lk 24:50–53 and Acts pp. 1:1–11 based on literary theories concerning beginnings and endings in literature. See above, pp. 74–75.

Pilgrim, Walter E. *Good News to the Poor: Wealth and Poverty in Luke-Acts.* Minneapolis: Augsburg Publishing House, 1981. Interprets the Lukan material dealing with possessions in terms of messages that the evangelist wants to send to both the rich and the poor. See above, pp. 99–100.

Richardson, Neil. *The Panorama of Luke.* London: Epworth Press, 1982. A general introduction to Luke's two works.

Sanders, Jack. *The Jews in Luke-Acts.* Philadelphia: Fortress Press, 1987. Offers exegetical commentary on the key passages in Luke-Acts dealing with the Jews and concludes that the third evangelist is anti-Semitic. See above, pp. 54–56.

Schottroff, Luise, and Wolfgang Stegemann. *Jesus and the Hope of the Poor.* Maryknoll, NY: Orbis, 1986 (German original, 1978). Attempts to recover the theme of Jesus' involvement with the poor that was present in the earliest Christian tradition and then traces the development of this theme in Q and Luke. See above, pp. 91–93.

Seccombe, David. *Possessions and the Poor in Luke-Acts.*

Studien Zum Neuen Testament und Seiner Umwelt. Linz, 1982. Suggests that Luke's treatment of this theme is an evangelistic address to persons whose devotion to wealth prevents them from accepting Christianity.

Sloan, Robert B., Jr. *The Favorable Year of the Lord: A Study of Jubilary Theology in the Gospel of Luke.* Austin: Schola, 1977. Studies the notion of Jubilee in Luke's theology, with emphasis on eschatological dimensions of the theme. See above, pp. 87–89.

Soards, Marion. *The Passion According to Luke. The Special Material of Luke 22.* Journal for the Study of the New Testament Supplement Series 14. Sheffield, England: JSOT Press, 1987. A redaction-critical analysis which concludes that the non-Markan material in this chapter can be attributed to Luke's own free composition or to his reliance on oral tradition rather than to the use of another source. See above, pp. 36–37.

Talbert, Charles H. *Literary Patterns, Theological Themes and the Genre of Luke-Acts.* Society of Biblical Literature Monograph Series 20. Missoula, MT: Scholars Press, 1974. An analysis of the formal patterns Luke uses in composing his two works and the implications these have for their interpretation. See above, pp. 38–39.

Talbert, Charles H. *Luke and the Gnostics: An Examination of the Lucan Purpose.* Nashville: Abingdon, 1966. Argues that Luke wrote his Gospel to serve as a defense against Gnosticism. See above, pp. 45–46.

Tannehill, Robert. *The Narrative Unity of Luke-Acts. A Literary Interpretation. Volume 1: The Gospel According to Luke.* Foundations and Facets. Philadelphia: Fortress Press, 1986. A study of Luke's Gospel as a continuous narrative, which tries to interpret all of the individual episodes in terms of the story as a whole. See above, pp. 11–14; 120.

Tiede, David L. *Prophecy and History in Luke-Acts.* Philadelphia: Fortress Press, 1980. Interprets Luke-Acts as an attempt to deal with the identity crisis faced by Jewish Christians following the destruction of Jerusalem. See above, pp. 48–51.

Tyson, Joseph. *The Death of Jesus in Luke-Acts.* Columbia, SC: University of South Carolina Press, 1986. A literary study of the way Jesus' death is presented in these writings, with special emphasis on the development and resolution of conflict between Jesus and his opponents.

Walaskay, Paul. *"And so we came to Rome." The Political Perspective of St. Luke.* Society for New Testament Studies Monograph Series 49. Cambridge: Cambridge University Press, 1983. Argues that Luke intended his work to serve as an apology to the Christian Church on behalf of the Roman empire, in the interests of improving Church/state relations. See above, pp. 84–85.

Wilson, Stephen G. *The Gentiles and the Gentile Mission in Luke-Acts.* Society for New Testament Studies Monograph Series 23. Cambridge: Cambridge University Press, 1973. An in-depth analysis of this theme which suggests that Luke's primary interest is to show that the incursion of Gentiles has taken place according to the will of God. See above, pp. 52–53.

Wilson, Stephen G. *Luke and the Law.* Society for New Testament Studies Monograph Series 50. Cambridge: Cambridge University Press, 1983. Argues that Luke conceives of the Jewish law as applicable only to Jewish people and, hence, as non-binding for Gentile Christians. See above, pp. 52–53.

**Collections of Important Articles:**

Cassidy, Richard J. and Philip J. Sharper, eds. *Political Issues in Luke-Acts.* Maryknoll, NY: Orbis, 1983.

Keck, Leander and J. Louis Martyn, eds. *Studies in Luke-Acts.* Philadelphia: Fortress Press, 1980 (originally published in 1966).

Mays, James Luther, ed. *Interpreting the Gospels.* Philadelphia: Fortress Press, 1981.

Talbert, Charles, ed. *Luke-Acts: New Perspectives from the Society of Biblical Literature.* New York: Crossroad, 1984.

Talbert, Charles, ed. *Perspectives on Luke-Acts.* Danville, VA: Association of Baptist Professors of Religion, 1978.

Tyson, Joseph, ed. *Luke-Acts and the Jewish People. Eight Critical Perspectives.* Minneapolis: Augsburg Publishing House, 1988.

**Some Commentaries:**

Caird, G. B. *Saint Luke.* Pelican New Testament Commentaries. Great Britain: Penguin Books, 1963.

Danker, Frederick. *Jesus and the New Age. A Commentary on St. Luke's Gospel.* Revised Edition. Philadelphia: Fortress Press, 1988.

Ellis, E. Earle. *The Gospel of Luke.* Revised Edition. The New Century Bible Commentary. Grand Rapids: Eerdmans, 1974.

Fitzmyer, Joseph. *The Gospel According to Luke I-IX* and *The Gospel According to Luke X-XXIV.* Anchor Bible. Garden City, NY: Doubleday, 1981, 1985.

Kilgallen, John. *A Brief Commentary on the Gospel of Luke.* New York: Paulist Press, 1988.

Marshall, I. H. *Commentary on Luke.* New International

Greek Testament Commentary. Grand Rapids: Eerdmans, 1978.

Obach, Robert E. with Albert Kirk. *A Commentary on the Gospel of Luke.* New York: Paulist Press, 1986.

Schweizer, Eduard. *The Good News According to Luke.* Atlanta: John Knox Press, 1984 (German original published in 1982).

Talbert, Charles. *Reading Luke. A Literary and Theological Commentary on the Third Gospel.* New York: Crossroad, 1986.

Tiede, David L. *Luke.* Augsburg Commentary on the New Testament. Minneapolis: Augsburg Publishing House, 1988.